ESTATE PLANNING
TRUSTS
FOR EVERYONE

First Edition Published in 2022 by
Porcupine Press
PO Box 2756
Pinegowrie, 2123
South Africa
admin@porcupinepress.co.za
www.porcupinepress.co.za

ISBN 978-1-9284-5595-0

Cover design and text layout by wim@wimrheeder.co.za
Set in 11 point on 16 point, Cambria
Printed and bound by dje Flexible Print Solution Pty Ltd

ESTATE PLANNING
TRUSTS
FOR EVERYONE

Discretionary Living Trusts – A legacy for generations

MERVIN MESSIAS

IMPORTANT NOTE

This publication is intended as a general guide only and does not constitute professional advice. The information, opinions and ideas which it contains are the author's and not intended to be a comprehensive study, or to provide legal advice, and should not be treated as a substitute for legal advice concerning particular situations. If the reader requires personal assistance or advice, a competent professional should be consulted before taking any action based on the information provided.

It is intended to provide helpful and informative material on the subject matter covered and is sold with the understanding that the author and publisher are not engaged in rendering professional services in this book.

For information, the author may be contacted at the following address:

Mervin Messias: BA, LLB (Wits) / TEP
(Trust and Estate Practitioner)
Address: 104, 11th Street, Parkmore,
Sandton 2196, South Africa
Contact: +27 11 783 0108
Email: mervin@mmtrustspecialist.co.za
Website: www.mmtrustspecialist.co.za

CONTENTS

FOREWORD

This user-friendly handbook is unique in that it unravels the mystique behind the discretionary living trust which is a pillar of personal asset protection and estate planning.

Whilst the handbook is primarily designed to create awareness of the importance of a correctly drafted trust deed, particularly in the context of estate planning, it also covers relevant aspects of the use of a trust in succession planning, disability planning, marriage, wills and curatorship.

This handbook offers the reader practical personal and estate planning solutions through the creative application of the discretionary living trust, based on the professional lifetime experience of Trust Specialist, Mervin Messias.

AH (Tony) Davey
BA (Natal), LLB (Natal), LLM (Unisa), H Dip Tax (Wits), Post Grad Dip Int Tax (UJ), Chartered Tax Adviser (SAIT), Fellow of the Institute of Chartered Secretaries, Advocate of the High Court.

ABOUT THE AUTHOR

Trust Specialist Mervin Messias has been a practising attorney for more than 40 years. The wealth of knowledge he has amassed across a broad range of legal disciplines has been skilfully channelled into developing a specialist Trust business.

His experience and reputation as a Trust Specialist are recognised both nationally and internationally. Renowned for his extraordinary depth of knowledge and proficiency in Trusts, his expertise includes Estate Planning, Wills and Tax incidental to Trusts.

In South Africa he has obtained BA LLB degrees from the University of the Witwatersrand, been a member of The South African Law Society Trusts and Estates committee, and a member of The Society of Trust and Estate Practitioners (STEP), where he served as chairperson of the Johannesburg branch for twelve consecutive years. He has also been a member of The South African Institute of Tax Practitioners (SAIT), which recognised him as a Master Tax Practitioner, and a member of The Fiduciary Institute of Southern Africa (FISA). He has lectured to and trained Attorneys, Accountants, Financial Advisors and given numerous presentations to members of the public on Trusts.

Internationally, he has been admitted as a Solicitor in England and Wales, Australia and New Zealand, as an

Attorney in Lesotho, and as a member of the National Network of Estate Planning Attorneys of the United States of America. He has also been admitted, by invitation, as an Academician of the International Academy of Estate and Trust Law.

ACKNOWLEDGEMENTS

I should like to dedicate this book to my three daughters, Lauren, Cara and Jade, each of whom has brought me joy, inspiration and pride.

Whilst the writing of this book represents the culmination of a personal lifelong ambition, by nature it is characterised by collaborative effort. Every individual involved has brought a different skill, expertise and perspective to the table and I should like to extend my heartfelt thanks to each of them.

Content and technical advice:
Advocate Anthony (Tony) Harding Davey.

Assistance with research and written content:
Sandra Cormie, DipEd (TTC).

Administrative Support:
Naajidah Dawood.

Proofreading:
Dinah Shapiro, BA (Wits), BA Hons (English) (Wits).

PREFACE

Trust planning is for almost everyone. It is planning that can change with us during our lives and beyond, and can provide for us and our loved ones. Without proper planning, our assets are exposed to risk and so are we, should mental or physical incapacitation become our reality at some later stage.

We all want our assets to be used to care for ourselves and our loved ones.

In my law practice as a Trust Specialist, I have assisted countless clients with their estate plans. They came from all walks of life: single and married; parents and grandparents; children and no children.

A Discretionary Living Trust is a unique legal entity. It was originally inherited from English Law and has been around for more than 1 000 years. Today it is widely used around the world, both onshore and offshore.

With a Discretionary Living Trust, we can create a legacy for generations. My mission is to improve the way estate plans are created. This book is intended to present, in easily understood language, a subject which is not widely understood or relied on, for those who are concerned about three essential planning concerns:

- Asset protection;
- Succession planning;
- Disability protection.

Wills and the cumbersome, protracted and costly deceased-estate-winding-up process have been relied on, but it has been recognised that Discretionary Living Trust planning is better suited to the modern society. It is no longer Will planning and tax planning for the wealthy. It is what I have espoused for my more than 40 years of practice experience.

In my consultations, I have always been asked 'What is a trust and what can it be used for?' and 'Why can't a simple Will be relied on?' A simple answer regarding a Will is that you have to die before it comes alive. It is for dead people. It cannot do anything to protect your assets, or avoid the protracted, complex and costly process of winding up a deceased estate or avoid the difficulty and costly curator process for disability (a Power of Attorney cannot be relied on as it is automatically terminated on mental disability).

This book is not intended to be a comprehensive text on the Discretionary Living Trust or in any way an academic text, but merely an introduction, in non-legal language, to the concept, to enable you to seek expert advice and to be sufficiently informed to be able to require meaningful advice for your estate plan.

I do not believe you should attempt to plan your estate by yourself. A little bit of knowledge can be very dangerous with regard to the estate-planning process. On the other hand, some knowledge can go a long way, if it is used to select and work with a professional advisor. In my opinion, you should always look for a specialist who practices in the area of estate planning to the exclusion of most other matters.

When should you start your trust planning? The clear answer, if you have not already done so, is *as soon as possible*.

1.
ARE YOUR AFFAIRS IN ORDER – GOOD SENSE OR NO(N)SENSE?

Unfortunately, dying is not optional. We live our lives, do the best we can, learn to love (and let go), experience highs and heartache, adjust our plans and refocus our priorities… You know the drill.

Why wait until you are old to think about the legacy you would like to leave, or to whom you could safely entrust it? Life involves acquiring things deemed important to making the most of every life stage – like an education, a career, a family, a home, savings. Some of it is material; much of it is experiential. The point is, the earlier you start with the material aspect, the greater the likelihood of finishing stronger.

You may be young, busy living your life, and the dismal subject of death is furthest from your mind. Or perhaps, you're the proverbial ostrich gripped by a fear of death? Neither approach ends well.

Money can destroy families and death is often the catalyst that brings it to a head. It need not be this way. The secret lies in competent Estate Planning.

Contrary to popular belief, attorneys do not enjoy

the misery of others, but they do benefit from ill-preparedness and the fallout that lands in their laps. Few take pleasure in wading through the adversarial storm of warring family members or the devastation that follows when people die intestate.

Specialists in Estate Planning, Trusts, Wills and Tax offer a proactive and more secure alternative that helps mitigate all the above. When you are properly prepared, your express wishes are carried out to the letter so that your assets do not land in the wrong – or undeserving – hands.

Estate Planning, Trusts and Wills focus on the people closest to you: partners, children, grandchildren, favourite family members and close friends. It means you get to nominate each Beneficiary (individuals and charities) and what assets you want included (life assurance policies, savings, property, business interests, family heirlooms and so on). It cements your and their financial security in life and beyond the grave. The amount in your estate is not the issue. The issue is securing what you have accrued for the people you determine as Beneficiaries, and no one else.

Apart from costly taxes, there are prescribed procedures with red tape and Courts of law that only a group of specialists know how to navigate efficiently. Few people understand the complexity of this process or the time frames.

Obviously, there are set-up costs for Estate Planning, Trusts and Wills, but it boils down to less now or a lot more later!

Since each client is unique, there is no one-size-fits-all approach. You want a neat, clear, and carefully structured package that is exclusively yours; one that provides complete peace of mind. A chaotic paper trail of instructions that lacks clarity and direction holds all the charm of a hand grenade.

Estate Planning is for all South Africans with assets and liabilities, regardless of race, gender, religious persuasion, age or means. This field of law is so intricate that inexperienced practitioners may unwittingly create a Trust with more holes than a commercial fishing net. Easier to fix before than after death, so you are urged to take the matter seriously and deal with it as a matter of urgency.

2.
ESTATE PLANNING IS ABOUT MORE THAN MONEY

Estate Planning is more about people than money. It is about securing the futures of those you love with a carefully structured legacy that leaves no room for uncertainty. Think of it as an expression of gratitude for the way in which certain individuals have added value to your life and helped you live it well.

Assets and immovable property generally spring to mind, but Estate Planning is also about taxes which, by their very nature, involve people like lawyers and accountants. Expert Estate Planning can help mitigate the tax implications by involving a team of advisors who can accomplish things that most people do not understand.

Proper planning is time and money. The complexity of sorting out someone's financial affairs when they die can be extremely daunting. If your legacy is well organised and finely documented, the process will be a lot kinder and more straightforward. It will also help eliminate unnecessary time delays spent chasing elusive documents.

Estate Planning allows you to identify and accomplish

goals that are personally important in life and after death, since it can be structured to define and maintain a lifestyle consistent with your asset portfolio.

Prioritise your commitment to make ongoing material provision for those that matter most to you, both in the short- and long-term, in life and after death.

What should be important to you when it comes to fulfilling your wishes:

- To give your property to whom you want, in precisely the way you want.
- For your Beneficiaries to receive their inheritance when you wish them to receive it.
- To save tax.
- To avoid, or at least reduce, attorneys' fees and court costs.
- To dispense with a lot of red tape that prevents your objectives from being accomplished expediently.

An estate plan should be your legacy, your way.

Learn how to expand your planning horizons. First, crystallise your thinking, then research experts in the field of estate planning, and be guided by their professional input. Engage the person of choice in a meaningful dialogue that culminates in a plan that will achieve your objectives and eliminate confusion or complications.

The 'why do today what I can put off until tomorrow?' mindset is ill-advised, as death has no respect for time or good intentions. You are urged to consider Estate Planning as mandatory, whether you have much material worth, or some.

Estate Planning is becoming more complex every day, because it encompasses so many different disciplines and forms. This introduction is designed to get you thinking about the diverse opportunities for strategic Estate Planning – planning to make your life more enjoyable while you are alive and for your Beneficiaries after you pass on, planning that can protect your assets from attack by a third party, planning to escape some of the potential problems associated with an untimely disability, and planning to reduce certain taxes.

Avoid a disorganised, convoluted, and muddied wasp's nest of instructions. It is not the most loving legacy to leave anyone – and it may not hold up in Court if contested!

Plan the right way, right away.

3.
WHAT IS A DISCRETIONARY LIVING TRUST?

Trusts are not new to South Africa, but since they have long been associated with the upper echelons of society, they have become somewhat shrouded in an elitist mystique, to the detriment of the layperson.

Trusts are available and advantageous to anyone with assets. They are a legal concept introduced to South Africa by English law in the 19th century. Of necessity, they have become reconciled with Roman Dutch law and remain a work in progress in terms of the law.

Apart from the application of case law, trusts were initially governed by the Trust Moneys Protection Act, No. 34 of 1934. However, the need for more extensive checks and balances in Trust matters led to the promulgation of the Trust Property Control Act 57 of 1988. This enabled the Master of the High Court to exercise a supervisory role in Trust matters, and to provide some legal muscle in the event of non-compliance. Statutory applications – such as the Income Tax Act, the Company Law Act, the Financial Institutions Act and the Deeds Registry Act – also help regulate the powers and limitations of Trusts.

There are different types of Trusts, each with a specific purpose determined by the Founder. They are all governed by the Trust Property Control Act. However, where Testamentary Trusts are governed by the *law of testation and succession*, Discretionary Living Trusts fall under the *law of contract*.

Be warned, Trusts are not a means to mask illegal activities for spurious gains.

The Trust that is the prime focus of this booklet, a Discretionary Living Trust, is a contract for the benefit of a third party. It does not possess legal personality. Revolutionary by nature, it has been widely accessed and utilised in the United States of America, as a solution to the potential shortcomings and pitfalls associated with stand-alone Wills and other types of Trusts, such as Testamentary Trusts (which only come into effect when the Founder dies).

To date, the Discretionary Living Trust (*inter vivos* Trust) has received little public exposure, which has kept it largely under the radar – an injustice in light of the extensive benefits it offers.

A Discretionary Living Trust is an extremely positive lifestyle choice, as this booklet will demonstrate. The legal term '*inter vivos*' means 'during the lifetime'. Since it is not affected by the Founder's death, it avoids estate duty.

A Discretionary Living Trust grants asset ownership to the Trustees, who have been carefully selected by the Founder for their business acumen, administrative skills and integrity. It is a contractual agreement whereby they hold and administer the Trust assets for the benefit of the Beneficiaries. They have a fiduciary responsibility that excludes any personal access to, or enjoyment of benefits themselves.

This safeguards against any abuse of Trust funds, because Beneficiaries do not have an automatic right to access the Trust funds. They are required to apply and motivate for the release of funds through the Trustees. The Trustees then exercise their discretionary powers, the scope of which should be clearly defined by the Founder in the Trust Deed.

A Discretionary Living Trust need not have a time limit. It allows for continual succession with benefits passed down from one generation to the next.

Mercifully, assets held in a Discretionary Living Trust are also protected from the consequences of misfortune – such as insolvency, divorce or death.

A Discretionary Living Trust stands on three core pillars:

- Asset protection;
- Succession planning;
- Disability protection.

It espouses continuity of function and benefits as its pivotal advantage, since it is fully operational during the Founder's lifetime, and continues without interruption when the Founder dies. This gives it an incalculable advantage – the family is free to mourn the passing of the Founder, without disruption to benefit flow. To remove financial anxiety from a grieving family is an especially caring gesture.

The Trustees remain in the driver's seat, keep the Trust on course, and meet the Founder's objectives. Business as usual.

Put simply, it is a legal contract, in which the Founder maps the way forward with absolute precision. The Trust Deed is the map. It eliminates confusion or dispute regarding which road to take. It is able to make provision for any unexpected detours and keep the Beneficiaries from straying into any danger zones, ensuring that no one arrives at a dead end.

A Discretionary Living Trust is more about enjoying the journey than simply arriving at a final destination.

4.
THE FORMATION OF A DISCRETIONARY LIVING TRUST

THE BASIC CONCEPT OF A TRUST

The person seeking to form the Trust is referred to as the Founder (or Settlor). The other two parties to a Trust are the Trustees and Beneficiaries. The premise of a Discretionary Living Trust is that the Founder must enter into a contract with the Trustee/s. The contract requires the Founder to 'make over' the assets as determined by the Trust Deed to the Trustees, to administer for the sole benefit of the Beneficiaries. The Trustees are required to be properly authorised by the Master of the High Court.

FOUNDER'S CHECKLIST BEFORE PROCEEDING

1. You have assets you would like to grow in value and keep out of reach from unwelcome third parties.
2. You have a succession plan in mind and want to create a tamper-proof, tax-efficient blueprint for your Beneficiaries.
3. You would like your financial and specific personal affairs controlled by a team of administrative experts,

who are unlikely to be swayed by family emotion or discord during your lifetime, and after you pass.

4.   You want to legally avoid being liable for some taxes.

5.   You are keen to avoid the inevitable delays associated with winding up an Estate and make provision for an uninterrupted flow of benefits to your Beneficiaries when you pass.

REQUIREMENTS FOR THE FORMATION OF A DISCRETIONARY LIVING TRUST

A Trust must have a *lawful* purpose and comply with the laws of contract, the terms of the Trust Property Control Act, common law and good business practice. It cannot be formed to hide assets from the relevant authorities, act as a mechanism through which to launder ill-gotten gains or become the 'alter ego' of the Founder.

The Founder must have a bona fide and conclusive *intention* to create the Trust, based on its contractual nature between the relevant parties. The Founder and the Trustee/s must be in agreement with one another regarding the *intention* of the Trust, as the Founder will be required to transfer ownership of specified assets to the Trustee/s, to administer on behalf of the Beneficiaries. This *intention* imposes an obligation on the Trustees to act as 'owners' of the assets without receiving any of the benefits themselves. It clearly separates ownership from enjoyment. The *intention* of the Trust will also determine whether the Trust is legally legitimate, or dressed up as some other legal entity – like a partnership or simulated (sham) Trust.

An *intention* without a contract defining the *obligation* is essentially pie in the sky. An *inter vivos* Trust must show mutual consent between Founder and Trustee/s, or it will have no legal effect. The contract must create the *obligation* it intends to impose on the Trustees, because the Trustees will be required to comply with the terms and conditions determined by the Founder in the Trust Deed.

The Trust *property* must be clearly defined. It may comprise any asset or group of assets, movable or immovable, tangible or intangible – anything from cars to copyright, business assets to shares or farms to family heirlooms.

The Trust *object* must also be defined with reasonable certainty. The *object* is the person or entity chosen to receive benefits from the Trust and must be determined by name. A Trust without named Beneficiaries is invalid. The Founder may want to give the Trustees the right to appoint other Beneficiaries, in which case this clause must be included in the Trust Deed at time of drafting, or by amendment later. The Trustees will be required to follow the legal protocols to validate any decisions to this effect. New *objects* must be legitimate and have no illegal or immoral purpose. An impersonal *object* is valid only if it is charitable or for the public benefit.

By nature, Trusts may stray into grey areas, which is why poor drafting and ignorance are cited as the two main reasons a Trust might fail.

An 'alter ego' Trust, common to Family Trusts, bears

all the hallmarks of 'business as usual', when in fact, it defeats the rationale of a Trust (which is to entrench a balance of power by including all trustees in the decision-making and implementation of resolutions by majority or unanimous vote, as may be required by the Trust Deed). An 'alter ego' Trust is exploited by the Founder, so that he or she can continue to wield influence on the running of the Trust for his or her own benefit. It is used as a means to maintain control and enjoyment of the assets, by running roughshod over the Trustees, and exerting his or her authority as if nothing has changed.

Therefore, the potential Founder is required to think carefully about the *intention* and objectives he or she hopes to achieve by forming a Trust and take those ideas and concerns to a specialist of choice. The intention and objectives are centred around Asset Protection, Succession Planning and Disability Protection. The Founder has to accept that he or she will not be in control of the assets in the Trust and that control will be vested in the Trustees, acting jointly. The Founder could be one and thereby have a say, as a Trustee, regarding Trust decisions.

Here, the specialist's legal knowledge, experience and foresight will prove invaluable on multiple levels. Over years of practice, they have learned how to set out the terms and conditions of the Trust to cover essential clauses, as well as make individualised refinements that allow for the complexities and scope required to draft a Trust that fits the Founder's specific objectives and *intention*. It should be structured with some flexibility to accommodate any changes in personal circumstances or the law, so that it will continue to function as the Founder intended, both during his or her lifetime and after death.

The law makes it possible for the Founder to be a Trustee and/or a Beneficiary, but *never the sole* Trustee and Beneficiary. Once the Founder becomes a Trustee, his or her role as Founder may cease to exist (unless a provision in the Trust Deed states otherwise). He or she is then obliged to function as a Trustee with all the fiduciary administrative responsibilities required by law. There is no special status conferred on a particular Trustee, even if he or she was the Founder.

The Trustees are required to submit the Trust Deed to the Master of the High Court for authorisation and a reference number, and obtain the Letters of Authority that empower them to act as Trustees.

5.
THE PARTIES TO A DISCRETIONARY LIVING TRUST

There are two parties to a Trust, the Founder and the Trustees, both of whom are signatories to the Trust. Beneficiaries are not necessarily signatories to the Trust, unless they are also the Founder or a Trustee.

However, someone has to get the ball rolling and initiate the process, and that someone is the Planner. He or she will have personal reasons for wanting to create a Trust.

The Planner is required to crystallise his or her thinking with respect to the *who, what, why, when* and *how*. Once established, they take their plan to a Trust Specialist for legal advice so that the Trust Deed can be discussed and structured as envisaged.

Whilst the Planner is responsible for instigating the Trust, he or she may choose not to be the Founder. This person is not a legal party to the Trust unless he or she chooses to continue being involved as the Founder or a Trustee. However, it is *not* legal for a person to be the only Trustee and the only Beneficiary, as there must not be a blurring between ownership and enjoyment.

Subsequent to the trust being created, any person who transfers assets into the Trust is referred to as a funder. This person may, or may not be, the Planner or Founder. Any third party may make a donation to the Trust.

FOUNDER

The Planner often chooses to be the Founder. When this is not the case, the Planner may ask someone else to be the Founder. It is also possible to have more than one Founder, persons who act jointly to create a Trust.

When the Discretionary Living Trust is drafted, the Founder must demonstrate clear intention to enter into an agreement with the Trustees for the benefit of Beneficiaries. He or she is required to be *divested of all or part of the legal proprietary right and power of control over the Trust property (as determined in the Trust Deed) and relinquish ownership in favour of the Trustees.*

A Founder has no legal right of enjoyment of Trust property (unless he or she is also a Beneficiary) and no power of control (unless he or she is also a Trustee).

Once the Trust has been drafted, approved and signed by the Founder and Trustees, the Founder generally plays no further role, unless a certain function is required of him or her, as determined in the Trust Deed. If the Founder is a Beneficiary, he or she may receive distributions from the Trust during his or her lifetime.

When the Founder becomes a Trustee, he or she is able to participate in the running of the Trust *as a Trustee.* This affords him or her the opportunity to continue being instrumental in the running and outcomes of the Trust and guide his or her legacy to fruition. That said, even if this person was the Founder, he or she cannot claim any special status or reserve any special powers as a Trustee and cannot, therefore, throw his or her weight around and impose unilateral decisions on fellow Trustees.

TRUSTEES

The Trustees are chosen by the Founder to take (non-beneficial) ownership of the Trust assets and act fairly with respect to the Beneficiaries. There is no limit to the number of Trustees the Founder may appoint. However, a minimum of two is advisable. Their role is completely dissociated from their private circumstances so that there can be no conflict of interests. See Chapter 6 for information on their appointment, role and powers.

BENEFICIARIES

Again, these are determined by the Founder and have to be clearly identified in the Trust Deed. It is possible to add new Beneficiaries and disinherit others by amendment. In a Discretionary Living Trust, the Beneficiaries do not own or control any Trust assets. They receive the benefits at the discretion of the Trustees. However, once they have accepted any benefits from the Trust, their consent will be required to effect any changes to the Trust Deed, as in law they become regarded as parties to the Trust Deed, notwithstanding that they have not signed the Trust Deed itself. They do not become owners of the assets in a Discretionary Living Trust and remain as discretionary

Beneficiaries. They are not like shareholders of a company.

Trusts are complicated legal entities. If it is your intention to create one, think carefully about the how, what, where, when and why, because it is a powerful and deeply personal legal entity that needs to be 'just right'. Choosing the right Trustees is an important step, as the next chapter will explain.

6.
TRUSTEES: CUSTODIANS OF WEALTH AND WELFARE

PART ONE:
CHOOSING AND APPOINTING TRUSTEES

Appointing Trustees is a serious business. With respect to a Discretionary Living Trust, they will be required to assume non-beneficial ownership and control of Trust property. Choosing the right people requires great wisdom and forethought.

A Trust Deed is regarded as a constitutive charter. This places a fundamental duty on Trustees to act within all applicable statutory provisions, the principles and rules of common law and the terms and parameters determined by the Trust Deed.

Desirable characteristics of a Trustee include the following:

- Requisite knowledge as it applies to related laws and performance expectations.
- Commitment to the principles of good governance, showing up for meetings and adding value to the decision-making.

- Integrity and honesty.
- Competence based on business acumen and administrative skills.
- Diligence.
- Impartiality.
- Financially secure and able to compensate the Trust for any errors made. Alternatively, to ensure that they are indemnified in the Trust Deed.
- Situated in the area where the Beneficiaries and assets are located.
- Have a good relationship with the Beneficiaries.

The circumstances that should disqualify someone from holding office as a Trustee:
- Anyone with private monetary problems.
- Has been sequestrated, liquidated or placed under judicial management.
- Has a history of substance abuse.
- Has a history of mental instability.
- Has a criminal record.
- Minors.
- Has a conflict of interests.
- Has a grudge against any other parties to the Trust.

Trustees can be individuals or corporations. Trust law allows for the Founder to become a Trustee, but not the sole Trustee.

It is advisable to have a combination of several individuals (or professional Trustees) to obtain a balance of qualifications and establish a comprehensive and informed input base, one that fosters a climate of account-ability – as much to one another, as to the Founder and Beneficiaries of the Trust. Some insider information gleaned over years from an association with the Founder is advantageous, so close friends that fit the profile may also be prime candidates.

After the list of candidates has been determined, each candidate should be approached individually. The potential appointment needs to be discussed with each one so that they are comfortable serving in the role of Trustee and doing the necessary (and often onerous) work to achieve the Founder's objectives. It is not every-one's cup of tea!

Before accepting the appointment, these persons must be aware of the duties and obligations imposed on Trustees, and be satisfied that they are in a position to accept the appointment. By this, they believe that they are a suitable candidate in terms of experience, expertise and availability.

Conversely, before accepting the appointment, they would be well advised to do some due diligence of their own.

- Consider the true objective of the Trust and be satis-fied that there is no improper purpose, for example, impending divorce or sequestration.
- Since the law does not tolerate ignorance as an excuse, check the Trust Deed for liability clauses and insurance cover.
- Request financial statements, records of Trustee meetings and resolutions, the register of Trust assets

and written assurance that the Trust is registered as a taxpayer.
- Remuneration policy.

Trustees are required to:
- Act in a fiduciary capacity – that is, they are legally obliged to act in the best interest of another, these being the Beneficiaries of the Trust.
- Be responsible for ensuring the Trust property serves its purpose – to run the Trust as determined by the Founder in the Trust Deed for the benefit of the Beneficiaries.
- Act as office bearer with the task of administering the Trust without enjoyment of any of the benefits (unless the Trustee is also a Beneficiary).
- Make prudent decisions when there is no clear-cut alternative.
- Act as an agent with the power, accountability, and liability inherent in the role.

Out of curiosity, you may now be wondering if you know of any suitable candidates in your own circle! Let us take a look at the pros and cons of personal or corporate Trustees.

Personal Trustees
Advantages:
- They will often serve for little or no fee. If required, fees are generally negotiated.
- They are free from corporate processes, which facil-

itates decision-making and action.
- They are usually known and trusted by the Beneficiaries.

Disadvantages:
- They may not have the necessary objectivity or experience. However, where knowledge or skills gaps exist, they are within their rights to employ people to advise them – for example, accountants or financial advisors.
- They may die, become incapacitated, greedy or be sequestrated.

Removing them from office for failing to follow the rules or act in the best interests of the Beneficiaries could incur unwelcome legal costs.

Corporate Trustees
Advantages:
- Objectivity.
- Professional wisdom and expertise based on experience.
- If they die, become incapacitated or sequestrated, their obligations will be assumed by another nominee within the corporation.
- They may be regulated by government agencies.
- They have the resources to make good any errors or mistakes.

Disadvantages:

- They charge a fee for their services, usually calculated as a percentage of the income earned by the Trust property over the period of a year and on capital distributions. However, this is subject to change and sometimes a minimum, fixed fee is applied. Some institutions may also charge a termination fee.
- They are often perceived as uncaring because they are outside the inner circle and mandated to make unemotional decisions.
- They may not be the best choice for an Estate that consists mainly of immovable property and/or a family business.

Trustees often work as a team with duties allocated to individuals, usually aligned to their specific field of expertise. They are required to invest in proven investment portfolios on a conservative basis, since speculative investing is deemed improper.

It is recommended that the Trust Deed make provision for successor Trustees, as a serving Trustee could die unexpectedly or become incapacitated in some way. In the case of appointing inexperienced successor Trustees like spouses or adult children, it is advisable to engage the services of an Estate Planning specialist to educate them in their roles as Trustees so that they fully understand their function and add value to the management process.

The Founder is required to act with extreme prudence and inner circle savvy when selecting Trustees. It is not a job for the fainthearted and definitely unsuited to anyone with a penchant for megalomania, dithering, whimsy or petulance.

PART TWO:
ADMINISTRATION OF TRUSTS

The Trustees are the glue that holds the entire Trust plan together. They are required to keep it on course in order to meet the Founder's objectives. The prescribed legal principles are lengthy and complex, but this section endeavours to simplify them.

The three main principles that govern the administration of a Trust:

1. Trustees are obliged to follow the instructions laid out in the Trust Deed and ensure that in so doing, no laws are breached. Any departure from instruction or legal parameters that incurs loss may involve the Trustees in liability and oblige them to make good such loss, even if they were acting in good faith.

2. Trustees must act with care, diligence, and skill as one governing the affairs of another. The expectation is that they should take even greater care than they would of their own property.

3. Trustees must exercise discretion in all matters.

Administrative duties

Before the Trustees can proceed with their administrative duties they have first to obtain and lodge the original or a certified copy of the Trust Deed with the Master of the High Court. The Trust Register contains the name of the Trust, the registration number and the date of registration. A Master's file which contains a copy of the Trust Deed and the names of all the Trustees and Beneficiaries is opened for each Trust. Neither the Trust Deed nor the Master's file is open to the public.

Next, they must have their appointment as Trustees authorised by the Master. Each Trustee is required to furnish security to the Master, unless the Master chooses to exercise his or her discretionary power and exempt security compliance by a Trustee.

Only then, can they get down to business.

They have a duty to act jointly and as such, decisions require either a majority or unanimous vote. In the event of a dispute, their fiduciary commitment obliges them to find common ground, as a properly run Trust leaves no room for 'puppet' Trustees. Their office requires them to act independently – that is, without taking instruction from, or being bullied by the Founder, Beneficiaries or other Trustees.

These are the duties of a Trustee in a Discretionary Living Trust:

1. The Trustees *act together* to take *control and possession* of Trust property. In some cases, their duty may only be to deliver it to the Beneficiary, in which case possession falls away.

2. To acquire ownership of the Trust property. The property must be vested in someone and unless the ownership can be regarded as vesting in the Beneficiaries, the Trustees assume ownership. With

respect to a Discretionary Living Trust, the latter applies.

3. Trustees are required to keep strict accounting records and financial statements that comply fully with The Trust Property Control Act, common law and the Trust Deed.

4. They are expected to appoint either an auditor or an accounting officer.

5. They must keep detailed records of Trustee meetings and resolutions.

6. They are accountable to the Master for their record keeping and administrative performance, and must be able to account for and deliver, upon request by the Master, any book, record, account or document in connection with the administration and disposal of Trust property.

7. They are obliged to keep a proper and detailed asset register that clearly identifies Trust property, maintains a record of the nature of the Trust assets (property, money and shares) as well as their precise location and the monetary value of each (historic cost and market value by way of a note to the balance sheet). This must be stated from an accounting and tax perspective. The issue of liquidity and insolvency must be addressed and they are required to ascertain what is necessary for distribution and how that might best be determined.

8. To conserve Trust property in a manner that retains its value and, if possible, increases it. Hence, safe investments trump those of a speculative nature. In

general, the Trustees have a duty to keep the Trust assets properly invested in any of the investments authorised by the Founder in the Trust Deed, so that they serve the best interests of the Beneficiaries.

9. Keep all contracts concluded.

10. To open a bank account in accordance with Section 10 of the Trust Property Control Act 1988. This places a statutory duty on Trustees to deposit the money into a separate Trust account at an accredited banking institution.

11. To distribute income and capital subject to the directions prescribed in the Trust Deed. The Trustees may be required to pay the income and deliver or transfer the capital to the Beneficiaries.

12. To carry on a business if specified in the Trust Deed. It then becomes incumbent on the Trustees to run the business efficiently and not expose it to undue risk.

13. To account to any Trust Beneficiary in respect of the state of the Trust property. Subject to specific provisions in the Trust Deed, the Trustees will normally render annual accounts in which income and expenditure for a specific period are reflected. They should also record details of Trust Fund investments. Provided that this is done satisfactorily, a Beneficiary may not be entitled to demand any further account information.

14. To act impartially towards all Beneficiaries. That said, their discretionary powers may justify the application of unequal treatment to benefit other

> Beneficiaries considered to have the greater need.

15. The duties and powers of Trustees should be stipulated in the Trust Deed as the law does not currently define this aspect adequately.

16. Usually, Trustees may allocate income earned from assets or investments to pay for something specified, like education, but it is generally incumbent on them to grow the capital.

17. In the event the Trustees require professional advice, they have the right to consult or employ someone with the requisite knowledge and skill. However, this does not allow them to shirk their responsibility and employ another party to do the work they are able to do themselves.

18. May withhold income and/or capital from a Beneficiary if provided for in the Trust Deed.

19. Maintain safe custody of Trust documents (physical safekeeping and insurance).

It is clear that administering a Trust is not for the ignorant or fainthearted. The office of Trustee carries considerable responsibility and requires a specific set of skills bolstered by an eye for detail, wisdom in interpersonal relationships and an understanding of Trust law.

PART THREE:
POWERS OF TRUSTEES

Power, as observed through history, has been known to turn people from mice to maniacs. Granting power to anyone warrants considerable forethought. The Founder needs to reflect carefully on whom he or she will confer these powers and then determine the parameters in terms of scope and clarity. Trustee powers are broad and complex. This overview covers some general points. You are urged to consult a specialist for more depth and detail.

As Founder, you want people you can really trust to act in the best interests of your legacy and Beneficiaries; people who will use their powers to make sound moral and financial decisions. It is a fine balancing act that needs to empower the Trustees to do their jobs well, without overstepping any boundaries. That said, there are also reassuring legal checks and balances regarding their powers. These are defined – and limited – principally by the Founder of the Discretionary Living Trust Deed. A Trustee may exercise only those powers bestowed by the Trust Deed. These powers are also controlled by the Trust Property Control Act, which falls under the authority of the Master of the High Court.

Comprehensive powers of administration are usually recommended when the Trust Deed is drafted. These are created to help minimise any costly applications to court at a later stage for the granting of a required power not stipulated in the Deed.

Whilst Trustees enjoy discretionary powers with respect to how they can exercise a particular power, trusteeship remains a fiduciary position in common law and in the Trust Property Control Act. They have a legal duty of care, diligence and skill when tasked with managing the affairs of others.

The Founder really should seek legal advice when drafting a Trust Deed because a layman cannot be expected to know the latitude Trustees require in order to perform their function well. Often, crucial factors are overlooked because he or she knows no better, and inexperience may precipitate some troublesome consequences down the line. Scope, clarity, foresight, and flexibility are key.

Basic powers bestowed on Trustees are all subject to the terms and conditions determined to be in the best interests of the Trust. Examples are:

1. Full discretionary powers to deal with the Trust assets. This includes the terms and conditions of any transactions, investments, or loans they may be contemplating, like rates of interest or security requirements.

2. To open and operate one or more accounts with banks or other financial institutions of a similar nature in the name of the Trust fund, whether in South Africa or elsewhere. They also have the authority to close any such account/s.

3. To transfer from and receive money into the Trust, for example, deposits.

4. To acquire assets of any nature for the purposes of investment.

5. To let or hire assets of any nature.

6. To borrow money as they deem fit.

7. To lend money to any person, firm, company, or corporation.

8. To improve, alter, maintain, or repair any movable or immovable property belonging to the Trust.

9. To sell, exchange, donate, acquire, or otherwise dispose of any assets of the Trust.

10. To institute and defend legal proceedings of every description by or against the Trust and, to sign all deeds, Powers of Attorney, affidavits and other documents that may be required for such proceedings.

11. To exercise voting rights attached to any shares, stock, debentures, units, or similar assets.

12. To consult or employ experts in aspects of Trust administration that require specialised knowledge or skill.

13. To authorise the services of professional practitioners, independent contractors, and tradesmen to do work and render services for the incidental affairs of the Trust.

14. To pay from the Trust, debts incurred on behalf of the Trust by them in the exercising of their powers.

15. To decide to whom any moneys or assets due to be paid or given to any minor, are duly executed.

16. To grant to any Beneficiary the right to use Trust fund assets.

17. To recover and receive all debts, sums of money, goods and effects which are due, owing, payable or belong to the Trust.

18. To make donations for charitable, religious, educational, or other similar purposes.

19. To do all of the above in the execution of their

powers, whether in the Republic of South Africa or in any other part of the world.

20. If required, to register and administer the Trust in any part of the world as they may determine, subject to the requisite consents and authorities.

Trustees are obliged to act in the best interests of the Trust at all times. The detail is imperative. Since it is a fine balance, aim for precision and be guided by a specialist in this field.

7.
BENEFICIARIES OF A DISCRETIONARY LIVING TRUST

A Discretionary Living Trust is based on a fiduciary relationship that can make provision for the distribution of assets to Beneficiaries during the Founder's lifetime, after the Founder has passed away and to the generations that follow.

A Discretionary Living Trust Deed not only lays out the terms and conditions of who gets what, it clearly separates ownership (Trustees) from enjoyment (Beneficiaries). It needs to be structured in fine detail to cover multiple contingencies to protect it from the possibility of attack by third parties – with potentially dire consequences for the Trust and Beneficiaries.

The Founder is one party who can never be replaced. When the Founder is ready to have the Trust Deed drafted, he or she should consult an appropriately qualified Trust specialist. In it, the Founder can make provision for him- or herself as well as his or her Beneficiaries. The Founder may also serve as a Trustee and be a Beneficiary.

Trustees must have unbiased regard to the needs of all the Beneficiaries. They have the right to distribute income from assets on a discretionary basis and the authority to supplement income with capital.

Beneficiaries receive the enjoyment of the Trust assets – they may also have a *right to capital or income* – but their rights of enjoyment are *contingent*, that is, conditional. The distribution of assets is not an automatic right, it is at the discretion of the Trustees. Beneficiaries also get to enjoy *contingent rights* with regard to tax. Certain tax benefits accrue to a contingent right and protection is provided should any Beneficiary's estate be sequestrated. The Beneficiary is not a party to the contract until he or she accepts the benefits as a Beneficiary. Once a party, he or she acquires certain rights but *not ownership of the assets.*

How does the provision for amendments in the Trust Deed affect Beneficiaries? Ponder this for a moment.

Needs change over time and unforeseen circumstances often require expedient intervention. If the Trustees have not been empowered to make the required amendments, the process may be hampered to the detriment of the circumstance (such as a change to an investment), or Beneficiary (such as an urgent medical intervention).

Legally and practically speaking, the ability to amend a Trust Deed is of great value to a Beneficiary identified as such in the Trust Deed, because once he or she accepts any benefits from the Trust, it cannot be amended without his or her consent as well. As a Beneficiary, would you not want to have a say in the 'what, when and why' an amendment should be made?

A Trust specialist could advise the Founder on the scope the Trustees might require to administer the Trust more effectively, and enable them to make changes that would benefit the Beneficiaries.

Provisions of the Trust Property Control Act *offer Trust property protection* for Beneficiaries because the Act requires that Trust property be identified and kept separately from the personal estate of a Trustee.

Trusts are incredibly complex legal documents that define an individual's financial future and that of their Beneficiaries, and the layman cannot be expected to understand the intricacies of Trust law, or the nuances associated with it. It is all very well asking your conveyancing or divorce attorney friend for advice, but it would be like calling your psychiatrist friend when you're in cardiac arrest! Could you reasonably expect the relevant level of specialised expertise to achieve the outcome you require?

Anything that has the potential to obstruct the achievement of the Trust and prejudice the Beneficiaries should be carefully considered under the guidance and ingenuity of a specialist. As a Beneficiary, anything less has the potential to go pear-shaped when you least need it to!

8.
THE TRUST PROPERTY CONTROL ACT NO. 57 OF 1988

The Trust Property Control Act came into force on 31 March 1989, and was amended by the Justice Laws Rationalisation Act, No. 18 of 1996. It serves as an operational framework shaped by case law, and is monitored by the regional Masters of the High Court. The Masters hold jurisdiction in their designated regions and exercise their authority over the Trusts registered and accepted in those regions.

The purpose of the Act is to help define, regulate and govern the formation and administration of Trusts. Other statutes, such as the Income Tax Act (which includes Capital Gains Tax), the Transfer Duty Act, and the Estate Duty Act also apply to Trust law.

In this chapter, wherever possible, information contained in the Act has been *selected, condensed and simplified,* for ease of reference by non-legal persons. The Act can be accessed in full at www.gov.za/documents/trust-property-control-act-18-may-2015-1117.

DEFINITIONS

1. 'Trust'

In essence, this is the what, who and why of the Trust – that is, an arrangement through which the ownership in property of one person is made over or bequeathed to another person (a or b) via a Trust, to be administered or disposed of according to the provisions of the Trust instrument (also known as the Trust Deed) for the benefit of the person or class of persons designated in the Trust instrument, or for the achievement of the purpose stated in the Trust instrument:

a) To another person, the Trustee, in whole or in part, or

b) The Beneficiaries designated in the Trust instrument, which property is placed under the control of another person (the Trustee).

This does not include the case where the property of another is to be administered by any person as executor, tutor, or curator.

1.1 'Trustee'

Any person (which may include the Founder of the Trust) who acts as Trustee by virtue of an authorisation under section 6 and includes any person whose appointment as Trustee is already of force and effect at the commencement of the Act.

1.2 'Trust instrument'

A written agreement or a testamentary writing or a

court order according to which a Trust was created.

1.3 'Trust property'

This includes movable or immovable property, as well as contingent interests in property, which in accordance with the provisions of a Trust instrument are to be administered or disposed of by a Trustee. (A contingent interest does not take effect until a specific condition has been met.)

2. Certain documents deemed to be Trust instruments

If a Trust is created (or altered) by oral agreement, the Founder is required to record the creation or alteration in writing.

3. Lodgement of Trust instrument

The Trustee, before he can assume control of the Trust property, is required to lodge the original Trust instrument (and any subsequent amendments made to it) with the Master and pay the prescribed fee. Copies certified by a notary are also acceptable.

4. Notification of address

The Trustee must provide the Master with an address to which he can serve notices and process. The Master also requires 14 days' written registered notice of any change of address.

5. Authorisation of Trustee and security

Any person whose appointment as Trustee in terms of the

Trust instrument, section 7 or Court order, may only act in that capacity if authorised (in writing) by the Master. Such authority will not be granted unless this person has furnished security to the satisfaction of the Master for the faithful performance of his duties as Trustee, or he is exempted from furnishing security by the Master or court order.

6. Appointment of Trustee and co-Trustee by Master

If the office of Trustee cannot be filled or becomes vacant, and no such provision has been recorded in the Trust instrument, the Master shall appoint a person of his choosing, after consultation with as many interested parties as he deems necessary.

If the Master considers it desirable, he may also appoint a co-Trustee of any serving Trustee.

7. Care, diligence and skill required of a Trustee

A Trustee shall, in the performance of his duties and the exercise of his powers, act with the care, diligence, and skill which can reasonably be expected of a person who manages the affairs of another. The Trust instrument has no authority to exempt or indemnify a Trustee against liability for breach of trust where he fails to show the degree of care, diligence and skill as required.

8. Trust account

Whenever a person receives money in his capacity as Trustee, he shall deposit such money in a separate Trust account at an appropriate banking institution.

9. Registration and identification of Trust property

Subject to the provisions of specific Acts and the Trust instrument concerned, a Trustee shall:

- clearly identify the property he holds in his capacity as Trustee,
- register the Trust property in such a manner that clearly identifies it as Trust property,
- make an account or investment at a financial institution that clearly identifies it as a Trust account or Trust investment,
- make all such property identifiable as Trust property in the best possible manner,
- if the registration or identification of Trust property being administered by the Trustee does not comply with the requirements of the Act, the Trustee has 12 months to remedy the situation so that it complies with the provisions of the Act.

10. Separate position of Trust property

Trust property shall not form part of the personal estate of the Trustee, unless he is also a Trust Beneficiary and entitled to the Trust property.

11. Power of court to vary Trust provisions

If a Trust instrument contains any provision which brings about consequences which in the opinion of the Court, the Founder of a Trust did not contemplate or foresee and which,

- hampers the achievement of the purpose of the Trust instrument of the Founder, or

- prejudices the interests of the Beneficiaries, or
- is in conflict with the public interest,

the Court may, on application of the Trustee or any person who in the opinion of the Court has a sufficient interest in the Trust property, delete or vary any such provision as the Court deems just.

12. Report of irregularities

If any irregularity in the administration of the Trust comes to the notice of the person who audits the Trust account/s, he or she is required to report it to a Trustee in writing. If the irregularity is not rectified to the satisfaction of the person who reported it within one month, this person is duty bound to inform the Master.

13. Master may call Trustees to account

The Master, by written request, will call the Trustee to account for any irregularity reported to him, and require the Trustee to deliver to him any book, record, account, or document relating to the Trust. The Trustee will then have to answer truthfully any questions concerning the administration and disposal of Trust property put to him by the Master. The Master then has the right to appoint a suitably qualified person to investigate the matter and apportion costs for such investigation as he deems fit.

The Act takes this a step further and stipulates that if a Trustee fails to account or perform any duty imposed on him by the Trust instrument or by law, the Master or any person having an interest in the Trust property may apply to the Court for an order directing the Trustee to comply with the request or perform such a duty.

14. Removal of a Trustee

A Trustee may, on application from the Master or any person that has an interest in the Trust property, be removed from office by the Court, providing the Court is satisfied that the removal would be in the best interest of the Trust property. This includes:

- if he has been convicted of an offence in the Republic or elsewhere. The offence should have an element of dishonesty or a sentence of imprisonment without the option of a fine,
- if he fails to provide the required security within two months of being requested to do so by the Master,
- if his estate has been sequestrated, liquidated, or placed under judicial management,
- if he has been declared by a competent court to be mentally ill or incapable of managing his own affairs,
- if, under the Mental Health Act 1973 (Act number 18 of 1973 and amended in 1996), he has been detained in an institution or as a State patient.
- he fails to perform satisfactorily any duty imposed upon him by or under this Act, or comply with any lawful request of the Master.

15. Resignation by a Trustee

A Trustee may resign by notice in writing to the Master and the ascertained Beneficiaries who have legal capacity, or to the Tutors or Curators of the Beneficiaries of the Trust under tutorship or curatorship. (Tutorship usually refers to caring for the interests of a minor.)

16. Custody of documents

A Trustee shall not, without the written consent from the Master, destroy any document which serves as proof of the investment, safe custody, control, administration, alienation or distribution of Trust property before the expiry of a period of five years from the termination of a Trust.

17. Copies of documents

With respect to the estate of a deceased person, the Master (subject to request) may supply a certified copy of any document relating to Trust property under his control, to a suitably authorised person (like a Trustee or his representative) with an interest in such a document.

18. Remuneration of a Trustee

A Trustee shall in respect of the execution of his official duties be entitled to such remuneration as provided for in the Trust instrument or, where no provision is made, to a reasonable remuneration, which shall in the event of a dispute be fixed by the Master.

19. Access to Court

Any person who feels aggrieved by an authorisation, appointment or removal of a Trustee by the Master, or by any decision, order or direction of the Master made or issued under this Act, may apply to the Court for relief, and the Court shall have the power to consider the merits of any such matter, to take evidence and to make any order it deems fit.

20. Regulations

The Minister of Justice may make regulations regarding any matter which in terms of the Act is required or permitted to be prescribed.

I hope the reader finds this overview helpful, sufficient to grant peace of mind and the reassurance that the Trust Property Control Act has the muscle to enforce the procedural checks and balances that prevent abuse or mismanagement of Trust funds.

9.
AMENDING A DISCRETIONARY LIVING TRUST

An amendment to a Trust Deed is akin to adjusting the sails of a yacht, a form of redirection to accommodate a change for the benefit of achieving the Trust's goals.

Amendments are necessary adaptations triggered by unexpected situations. Examples include:

- A change of legislation, such as new or amended laws, changes precipitated by actual Court cases and High Court precedent rulings or new directives from the likes of SARS.
- A change of circumstance that the Founder could not have foreseen or contemplated, like provision for a special needs child.
- A change of Beneficiary (an addition or deletion), often initiated by divorce, remarriage, death or insolvency.
- A disagreement between parties.
- When the Trustees require less restrictive parameters to perform their duties more effectively.
- To overcome poor drafting that lacks sufficient clarity for the Trustees to act with any certainty.

- To remedy any flaws and mitigate any risks uncovered in an independent audit of the Trust.

The authority to amend a Trust Deed is found in statutory law, common law and the Trust Deed itself. If a Trust Deed is silent about amendments, statutory law and common law become the reference points. Discretionary Living Trusts enjoy contractual autonomy under the law of contract (the freedom to contract with whomever and on whatever terms), a consequence linked to the constitutional values of dignity, equality and freedom.

That said, there are three exceptional circumstances where the High Court may be called upon to intervene. The Courts generally strive to implement amendments that are aligned as closely as possible to the Founder's original purpose.

EXCEPTIONAL CIRCUMSTANCES

1. Dire necessity – that is, to remedy a situation where funds are required urgently: for example, to provide for the immediate welfare of a minor, cover legal costs relating to a Trust property, or make provision for a situation the Founder could not have foreseen.

2. Discriminatory provisions of public interest that are considered harmful to the moral welfare of society. Public policy is based on constitutional values that entrench the right to human dignity, freedom and equality. Any transgressions may lead to severability by the Courts – that is, the striking out of the offending provision in the Trust Deed. The excision

is usually undertaken in such a way that the rest of the Trust Deed is left intact.

3. When the object of a charitable Trust cannot be realised.

The introduction of the Trust Property Control Act 57 of 1988 was a turning point that gave the Courts more specific direction and power. Section 13 of the Trust Property Control Act now allows for judicial intervention in certain situations. The Act does not *replace* the Courts' power to amend Trusts per se, it allows them to *supplement* their common law power of amendment.

There are three specific situations that apply when the Courts are required to consider an amendment. Provisions in Section 13 of the Trust Property Control Act read as follows:

'If a trust instrument contains any provisions which brings about consequences which in the opinion of the Court the founder of a trust did not contemplate or foresee and which –

- hampers the achievement of the objects of the founder; or
- prejudices the interests of the beneficiaries; or
- is in conflict of the public interest,

the Court may, on application of the trustee or any person who in the opinion of the Court has a sufficient interest in the trust property, delete or vary any such provision or make in respect thereof any order which such Court deems just, including an order whereby particular trust property is substituted for particular other property, or an order terminating the trust.'

The Court cannot implement any changes or proceed without first considering the following aspects:

- The aforementioned three exceptional circumstances.
- The interested parties who have brought the application. This includes Beneficiaries and third-party Trust creditors.
- Whilst Courts have the power to amend, delete, terminate or apply any order to replace Trust property with other property, they cannot add anything deemed missing to the Trust Deed.
- If the contents are in conflict with the South African Constitution.
- Each case must be judged according to its unique circumstances.

IMMOVABLE PROPERTY ACT 94 OF 1965

Any Trust Beneficiary who has an interest in an immovable property that belongs to a Trust (but which is subject to a restriction), has the right to appeal to the Court to have the restriction removed if such removal is to the advantage of the applicant. The Act, on various grounds, enables the Court to remove or modify any such restriction. With respect to a Discretionary Living Trust, the Beneficiary would first apply to the Trustees, request the amendment and approach the Court only if the request was unsuccessful.

THE PARTIES TO A DISCRETIONARY LIVING TRUST AMENDMENT

The following parties, under common law and the Trust Deed, may make amendments to the deed.

1. The Founder, by agreement with the Trustees and the Beneficiaries who have accepted benefits.
2. The Trustees, by agreement with the Beneficiaries who have accepted benefits.

The scope of any amendments should be determined in the Trust Deed. If the Trust Deed is silent on amendments, an application to Court would have to be made.

It is always important to consider the scope given to the Trustees as specified by the Founder in the Trust Deed, because without the express provision to make amendments, the Trustees cannot assume that power. Any attempts to do so would be considered invalid.

When Trustees have authority and want to make an amendment to a Trust Deed, certain protocols should be closely observed. Firstly, in a properly constituted meeting of the Trustees, they should record the reasons and resolutions for the proposed amendment and if applicable, attach any record of advice offered on the subject by an attorney, accountant or fiduciary practitioner. Any previous amendments should also be taken into account and any Beneficiaries who have accepted their benefits, would also have to agree as a party to the amendment.

Trustees are warned against passing amendments

that constitute a novation (the bringing about of a new Trust) since this could trigger unwelcome taxes.

Amendments to a Discretionary Living Trust require a unanimous vote amongst the relevant parties before being lodged with the appropriate Master's office. Whilst amendments are considered valid from the time of signature (that is, by applicable parties), the Trustees are required to lodge the document with the Master. The Master will require the original signed Trust Deed amendment (or a certified copy thereof), together with the resolution.

A Discretionary Living Trust is able to overcome the potential complications more commonly associated with a Testamentary Trust, namely that the Trustees may be authorised to facilitate amendments that support general administrative function and decision-making, even after the death of the Founder.

Amendments to a Testamentary Trust are only possible while the Testator is alive. When the Testator dies, the opportunity to make any changes dies with him or her.

10.
TERMINATING A DISCRETIONARY LIVING TRUST

A Discretionary Living Trust has multi-generational benefits. Without time parameters, it can continue to exist for as long as it serves its purpose. However, termination may become necessary one day, owing to a number of factors:

- Upon application, by court order.
- Sequestration.
- The fulfilment (or failure) of the object of the Trust.
- The absence of Beneficiaries, either through death or renunciation of their rights as Beneficiaries. A Trust without Beneficiaries is null and void.
- The destruction of Trust property through no fault of the Trustees.
- The absence of Trust assets, such as, when all Trust assets have been distributed.
- The passing of a unanimous resolution by the Trustees. This first requires the Trustees to apply their fiduciary responsibility to the Beneficiaries (both current and future), to consider the rights of the Beneficiaries, the intention of the Founder, the

circumstances that justify the termination and the strategy regarding the disposal of any remaining Trust assets. In this instance, the Trust Deed should stipulate how the remaining assets should be dealt with – that is, a) whether they should be valued and/or sold or, b) how the residue should be distributed and to whom.

- The Trust Deed may have a resolutive condition that stipulates the Trust be terminated on a certain date or on the occurrence of a specific event – for example, the death of a named person or the attainment of a specified age of a particular Beneficiary.

The termination of a Trust requires the participation of certain parties.

- *The Court:* Only when ordering the termination of the Trust or, when Beneficiaries opposing the dissolution of the Trust approach the Courts for intervention.
- *The Founder:* That is, if the Trust Deed requires his or her involvement. A word of warning: if he or she has arranged a loan account against specific assets and receives the residue of the Trust assets without it being returned against his or her loan account, there could be tax consequences.
- *The Trustees:* As provided for in the Trust Deed, by unanimous agreement. Under common law, if the Founder is not excluded by the Trust Deed, he or she must reach a unanimous agreement with the Trustees.

- *The Beneficiaries:* Common law does not require the involvement of the Beneficiaries in the termination of a Trust.

Trustee responsibilities *prior* to applying to the Master to deregister the Trust:
- To comply with the Court order, if applicable.
- To prepare a final statement of the Trust's assets, their values and how they were determined.
- To adhere to the Trust Deed in terms of distributing, paying and giving over all Trust property to the Beneficiaries. The receipt of Trust property by the Beneficiaries must comply with SARS regulations.
- Settle all Trust liabilities and prepare a final statement that details how they were settled. If Trust liabilities exceed the assets, to start the liquidation process.
- Apply to SARS for deregistration of the Trust.
- Close the Trust's bank account and obtain a bank statement that reflects a nil balance.
- Cancel all insurance policy contracts and debit orders relating to the Trust.
- Make adequate provision from the Trust assets for the safe storage of the Trust documents for the specified *five-year period* following the termination of the Trust, as determined by Section 17 of the Trust Property Control Act.
- Ascertain and record the rights of all Beneficiaries.

In order to close the Trust file, the Master requires:

- A formal application to deregister the Trust.
- The original Letter of Authority.
- A request to cancel the Trustees' authorisation, signed by all the Trustees.
- The final financial statements of the Trust.
- Copies of final tax returns submitted to SARS that show all taxes due have been paid.
- Confirmation from SARS that the Trust has been deregistered as a taxpayer plus a tax certificate of good standing.
- An affidavit by the Trustees confirming that the Trust has been divested of all assets.
- Proof that the Trustees have done their duty and a) distributed all income and capital to the Beneficiaries and b) that the Beneficiaries have received their benefits (either by letters of acceptance or a letter of confirmation from the Trust accountant).
- A request to cancel the securities provided by the Trust Property Control Act, if applicable. (Once authorised, the Trustees have still to execute the cancellation.)
- The resolution that explains the reasons for terminating the Trust.
- Proof that the Trust's bank account reflects a nil balance.
- Contact names and details of the 'retiring' Trustees responsible for the safekeeping of the Trust documents over the designated five-year period, and for any future accounting responsibilities to the Master.

Once the Master has received all the necessary documentation, he is required to communicate his decision to the Trustees in writing, and inform them that the Trust is closed.

11.
WHY A DISCRETIONARY LIVING TRUST SHOULD BE PLAN A

Preparedness is the principle that underpins Estate Planning. Of great importance is the need to make provision for every life stage and unfortunately, the late life stage is often the scariest, and most costly. It is crucial that we understand the legal ramifications of diminished mental function in adulthood and how best to mitigate its impact, if ever it should strike. Let us look at just one possibility – dementia.

Here are three facts:

1. Dementia is not a natural part of ageing.
2. Worldwide, a new case of dementia is diagnosed every three seconds.
3. The health costs associated with dementia are escalating faster than the disease itself.

Young adults simply cannot conceive that one day their faculties may falter. And yet it happens, unwelcome as it is. And mature adults thought growing old would take longer, yet here it is…

Dementia is a growing public health concern globally

and as longevity is increasing, adequate service provision is not. Our unhealthy lifestyles (less exercise, poor diet, more stress and abuse of alcohol) increase the risk of developing some form of dementia. Even people in their thirties may begin to experience cognitive decline. Young or old, have you made provision for the debilitating possibility of dementia, PTSD, head injury and the like, however remote it may seem today?

We would all like to be treated with respect and dignity and not left in some arbitrary care facility where preferred lifestyle standards are not observed because of budget constraints. Plan ahead so that you will be able to afford a reasonable and professional standard of care. There is no guarantee that your family will take you in, as mental decline is an extremely stressful and difficult condition for unqualified people to handle.

If a Power of Attorney is your Plan B, best you sit down. It has absolutely no legal standing in a case of diminished mental function in adulthood. A Court of law will have to appoint a Curator to manage your life, assets, and affairs in general. (Refer to Chapter 19 on curatorship for more detail.)

The smarter option by far is Plan A! This solution includes a type of personal welfare insurance that can make advanced provision for temporary or permanent mental debilitation so that curatorship is avoided altogether. This alternative maintains the status quo without any unnecessary sacrifice of dignity, lifestyle, or control.

Unlike a Will, a Discretionary Living Trust can be

structured to cater for almost any contingency while you are alive so that, should mental debilitation become a reality, the Trustees you hand-picked have a duty to follow the instructions you determined in the Trust Deed. You should find this most reassuring!

Take any misapprehensions or uncertainties that may be keeping you from choosing the more secure, sensible option of a Discretionary Living Trust to a professional, and explore your reservations in depth.

12.
ASSET PROTECTION

Asset Protection is widely considered the most important pillar in Estate Planning.

The public often find it difficult to see beyond the costs of setting up and administering a Trust – and yes, it can be expensive. Common sense, however, suggests that it would be better to pay the set-up and administration costs as well as the taxes on deemed interest than to risk losing a chunk or all the capital you have worked hard to accrue, to an attack or claim. Growth protection is of paramount importance.

Vultures are opportunists that circle patiently for the meatiest carcasses, then pounce. When it comes to money, you do not even need to be dead (though you may wish you were!) to have them circling and gunning for the prize pickings you spent a lifetime slogging for, accruing and investing cleverly. You may even have amassed an enviable fortune, which is both empowering and risky, so much so, you keep your attorney on speed dial. Just in case.

Once there is an attack on your assets, you cannot scramble to create a Trust to protect them and avert the consequences of a claim. It is advisable to prioritise asset protection and create a Trust while the coast is clear. Why expose your assets to attack when there are ways to vulture-proof them? John Fletcher gives it to us straight: 'Of all the forms of wisdom, hindsight is by general consent the least merciful, most unforgiving.'

Property (art, jewellery, cars, etc), land, shares, insurances, investments, and accumulated wealth are all deemed to be assets. Therefore, there is much to be gained by having your Discretionary Living Trust Deed structured by an acknowledged specialist who knows all the potential traps, complications, and loopholes and how to handle them within the constraints of the law.

Consider this: if the Discretionary Living Trust does not comply with prevailing legal requirements, all protection falls away. It is estimated that around 90% of Discretionary Living Trust Deeds in South Africa are either faulty or invalid as a direct result of being drafted by someone who lacks the requisite specialist knowledge in the field. Consider medicine: you would not, for instance, expect your family doctor to perform your hip replacement surgery? Legal matters are no different.

Drafting the Discretionary Living Trust Deed takes time. How should you proceed?

1: GET YOUR ASSETS INTO A TRUST

Appoint a Trust Specialist to draft the Discretionary Living Trust Deed. The input of a Tax Specialist is a crucial component to drafting a Discretionary Living Trust Deed, as tax law is highly complex. The important thing is to keep your assets beyond the reach of any potential disgruntled parties – creditors, spouses, business partners, beneficiaries, and the like.

2: ADMINISTER THE DISCRETIONARY LIVING TRUST PROPERLY

When the Trust is created, it is required to be registered with the South African Revenue Services.

You appoint the Trustees – the custodians you choose will be people you know and trust, people who will have *your* best interests at heart. The Trustees must be authorised by the Master of the High Court. These checks and balances have a more personal and powerful significance.

The Trustees *cannot* act outside the Discretionary Living Trust Deed. They are legally required to open a bank account for the Trust as all monies received for the Trust – for example, dividends from shares – must be deposited into the Discretionary Living Trust account. An accountant must be appointed by the Trustees as they (the Trustees) are required to render annual tax returns on behalf of the Trust. The Trust is liable for tax on income generated and Capital Gains Tax if the Trust has disposed of any assets. (Refer to Chapter 15.)

The Trustees are also legally required to meet on a regular basis, minute every meeting and record any resolutions they pass. A majority vote is usually required but a unanimous vote may be required in other respects, for example, in regard to amendments. However, they cannot act until authorised at the outset by the Master of the High Court.

3: ALLOW FOR FLEXIBILITY

The Discretionary Living Trust Deed must be properly drafted to include some flexibility and accommodate unexpected contingencies. Any amendments need to be carefully drafted and lodged with the Master of the High Court. The services of an advocate are not required because there are no court costs.

Is it not important to your peace of mind that your hard-earned wealth is optimally protected so that when you pass, your Beneficiaries have immediate enjoyment of your material legacy with the minimum of fuss or interference? The thought of them struggling to access what you have left them because of complications, delays and red tape, is simply unconscionable and unnecessary.

13.
SUCCESSION
PLANNING

We have been staring down the barrel of the COVID-19 shotgun for much longer than we initially expected. What has been your response? Have you paused to consider if your affairs are in order, because a reality check is not necessarily a bad thing? Preparedness is key to staying ahead of any threat and it is fitting that you should have the final word regarding who your successors (heirs) should be. Legally formalising your legacy is of crucial importance on many levels.

Succession planning is about who should inherit your assets when you die. It is tricky by nature because it has the potential to be swayed by emotion. Without impartial, professional input and committing your intentions to a legally binding plan, things could go horribly wrong – and you may no longer be around to correct it! It is the last thing you want to mess up, simple at face value but fraught with potential pitfalls when it comes to execution and intended outcome.

Succession Planning sometimes necessitates particular considerations like special needs children, potential heirs with a history of substance abuse or those with a poor money management record. South Africa's 'sandwich generation', supporting ageing parents as well as immediate and extended family members, are in a difficult position. Proper succession planning offers the solution because it ensures uninterrupted and responsible provision for those who rely on you for financial support in the short, medium- and long-term.

A legacy is seldom straightforward. There are also people with no living family or children, others are part of a blended family or live in a relationship that has not been legally formalised. Every personal situation has a twist that requires specialised planning.

It can be tough deciding how to share your legacy equitably, but it boils down to who deserves what, why and under what conditions. Since an inheritance is a material expression of love and goodwill, why would you want it to be anything but a straightforward act of generosity devoid of complications?

You are urged to deal with specialists in this field, professionals with the requisite knowledge, reputation and business acumen honed over many years of experience. Someone you can trust implicitly because you need the assurance that your successors will receive optimal benefit and enjoyment of their inheritance as quickly as possible, with the minimum of fuss and without incurring unnecessary costs or taxes. The most successful and efficient succession plan is to be found in a Discretionary Living Trust.

But sadly, many people die intestate (without a Will). This is likely to mess up any succession plans that you may have been contemplating because the consequence of dying without a Will is that you will have missed the boat. It will have sailed, along with your good intentions. The Intestate Succession Act will kick in and the Master of the High Court will appoint an Executor. The Beneficiaries may not be who you wanted them to be, because familial black sheep, however distant, are notorious for crawling out of barns at the faintest whiff of money. If there is a minor (under the age of 18), any assets for the benefit of the minor will be paid into the Guardian's Fund to be controlled by some arbitrary civil servant. You may never get to rest in peace!

WHAT HAPPENS IF YOU HAVE A WILL?

An Executor is usually nominated at the time the Will is drafted. Since the Executor requires the Will to wind up your estate when you die, it can either be a person you trust or an impartial organisation, like a bank or insurance company.

The originator of the Will can amend it according to changing circumstances while he or she is alive but upon death, any changes will require the intervention of the Courts and they can only intervene under exceptional circumstances, and providing statutory authorisation to do so exists.

These exceptional circumstances include:
- Should a change in circumstance not foreseen by the Testator make the execution of a provision in the Will practically impossible or extremely unreasonable.
- The Testator based his or her bequests on erroneous

assumptions regarding his or her assets and liabilities.

- Strict adherence to the Testator's instructions will result in the failure of a bequest or thwart the Testator's real intention.
- The manner of execution as explained in the Will is either no longer possible or may result in great loss to his or her estate.
- The necessity of the case requires amendment.

Wills take at least one to three years to finalise because of the arduous legal processes. This means that the Beneficiaries may have delayed access to their inheritance and suffer hardship while the estate is being wound up. A recent newspaper article cites a backlog of such magnitude at key Master's offices, that there are delays in the winding up of deceased estates. The legal firms that handle deceased estates and the Beneficiaries of those estates are in a royal financial pickle and unable to proceed until the problem is resolved. That could take years.

A Discretionary Living Trust is a solution that will ensure your successors are not compromised by such disastrous external factors. Reconsider this additional benefit to creating a Discretionary Living Trust: It remains active even after the Founder has passed, which mitigates any delays, frustration and legal costs associated with a Will. (Take COVID-19 as an example: the Master's office closed owing to infections, and nothing could be processed.) Property can be dealt with immediately as it falls outside of the Administration of Estates Act 66 of 1965 and the inheritance process can be expedited.

It is a completely different legacy that does not require winding up an estate, it simply continues un-affected by such scenarios.

This Trust offers greater protection for the Founder during his or her lifetime (for example, disability protection) and the successors after the Founder's death because it is a living document governed by Trustees.

Unlike a Will, a Discretionary Living Trust does not die with the Founder, it is passed to the next generation as a work in progress. Therefore, estate duties do not apply. One can create a family of Trusts for individuals, each with Trustees as guardians of the funds. This helps prevent next-generation wars and gives individuals more control over their financial destinies and those of their families. After the Founder has passed, the Trustees retain the authority to make any necessary amendments in line with changing circumstances.

No two situations are alike. Consider your concerns and personal wishes carefully so that an entirely unique document can be structured to meet every specific concern, request, and directive. It also initiates a highly personalised relationship with your attorney, accountant or fiduciary consultant, one based on professionalism, trust, and confidentiality. Your choice of professional will serve as a reliable 'go-to' advisor and impartial sounding board for years to come.

14.
DISABILITY PROTECTION

We have looked at the first two pillars of Estate Planning – Asset Protection and Succession Planning. Now we look at Disability Protection. It is not something we like to look at lest we tempt fate or have to acknowledge that the ageing process (and its potential consequences) will eventually beset us all!

Disability protection is crucial because disabilities may strike randomly and unexpectedly, like strokes, heart attacks or motor accident injuries. Or they may take their time, like dementia, impaired sight or hearing, and diseases such as diabetes.

Having our affairs in order gives us a distinct advantage, both in the short- and long-term, because life has the uncanny habit of tossing ill-timed curve balls our way. Without such provision, you may find yourself at the mercy of family or friends, a rather onerous responsibility they may grow to resent. Also, a situation of this nature has practical and financial implications they may not be able to meet. So, the noble ideal of 'I don't want to become a burden to anyone' could very quickly become a reality. Being indebted to a third party is far from ideal; it could render you powerless and vulnerable.

But, if you have made contingency plans, then everyone will know how to proceed. The fruit lies in the way it is structured.

Disability Planning within a Discretionary Living Trust keeps the Founder in the driver's seat, even if he or she is incapacitated in some way later. Rock-solid planning will cover most eventualities, but the structuring process requires specialist advice based on experience and knowledge. Every nuance and situation needs to be considered and covered.

Despite the circumstances, having a designated plan within a Discretionary Living Trust has three key benefits:

- Disability Planning takes tough and emotional decisions away from distraught family members and plots the way forward as the Founder intended. This could be anything from what to do in the event of a debilitating accident or illness to how to manage a loss of mental capacity. It dispenses with potential family drama as well as meddlesome and conflicting input from well-intended outsiders.

- Disability Planning stipulates how the Founder would like to proceed in the event of incapacitation – temporary or permanent. It is clearly documented and not open to debate. To remove loved ones from having to take responsibility for traumatic decisions concerning your wellbeing is a profoundly loving consideration. It helps mitigate untold heartache and potential guilt.

- In a situation where family relations are strained

or you have no immediate family to make decisions for you, your Disability Plan will ensure you are protected. No aggrieved parties will be able to interfere or exact any 'pay back' they feel you deserve. How often have you heard of such people being tossed into some cheap and cheerless institution, and basically abandoned?

- When your Disability Plan is part of a Discretionary Living Trust, it may allow you access to funds should they be necessary for costly medical treatment or upkeep.

A Power of Attorney, however well-intentioned, is an alternative route with limited power and potential complications. You are trusting the appointed agent with your wealth and wellbeing.

- Firstly, it is often the action taken in response to a sudden onset problem. Diminished mental capacity is frequently the trigger, but it is illegal for a person who is already mentally incapacitated to sign a Power of Attorney.

- Unfortunately, South African law does not make provision for a durable Power of Attorney. This is a document which enables the agent to continue to make decisions for and on behalf of the person who has become mentally incompetent. A Power of Attorney becomes null and void once the subject is considered fully compromised mentally. Legally, a Curator should be appointed.

- If overseas accounts are involved, matters involving

Power of Attorney become complicated as each country has its own laws.

- Power of Attorney is not always readily accepted by third parties, like financial institutions.
- Should any physical incapacitation be temporary, and the party concerned would like to re-assume control of his or her affairs, the Power of Attorney should be cancelled and written communication to that effect sent to the parties who have a record of it.

In the absence of a Discretionary Living Trust, a Curator will be appointed to manage your affairs. You could find yourself on thin ice as the Curator is just one person without any personal connection to you, operating with limited checks and balances in place, now in charge of your affairs. He or she may not have your best interests at heart, and this presents a situation that is difficult to monitor. Abuse of power and funds is possible, and you will require a court order to cancel the Curator's services – which he or she may oppose. Since that represents an expensive and tedious legal process, curatorship should be avoided. Curatorship is covered in more detail in chapter 19.

A Discretionary Living Trust with a Disability Plan, on the other hand, offers a more secure outcome because it falls under the Trust Property Control Act, and gives the Master of the High Court the authority to hold the Trustees accountable.

A Discretionary Living Trust is a framework that holds the Trustees accountable to the law and to each other. In addition to their legal obligation to comply with the terms of the Trust Deed, a Declaration of Wishes, whilst not legally binding, is of great moral value when more personal decisions have to be made. A Curator, by comparison, holds all the cards.

The comprehensive document called a 'Declaration of Wishes' is a detailed, personal blueprint that provides explicit guidelines on how to carry out your wishes in multiple situations so that virtually nothing is left to chance.

You would do well to put your wealth and Disability Plan into a Discretionary Living Trust, pay the applicable taxes upfront and have the assurance that the Trustees you have appointed will take proper care of you as designated in the document.

A Disability Plan is uniquely yours and crafted with attention to detail. The protection provisions in the event of a disability are of great value for your peace of mind.

15.
DISCRETIONARY LIVING TRUSTS AND TAXES

Unlike a company or close corporation, a Discretionary Living Trust is not a juristic entity. It is classified *sui generis* (meaning, of its own kind). Therefore, it cannot be owned, transferred or sold. The assets can be owned, transferred or sold, but not the Trust itself.

By statute, income tax and capital gains tax are governed by the rules of attribution and distribution. In circumstances where the attribution rule does not apply, the distribution rule kicks in. In circumstances of no attribution or distribution, the trust itself is the taxpayer.

Special Trusts created for disabled persons and minors are taxed at a reduced rate.

The value of utilising a Discretionary Living Trust as part of an estate plan is incalculable. Legitimate tax breaks are just one benefit. Since these taxes are complex and subject to variation, the following information is provided as a *general overview*. The statistics mentioned are current to 2021. For greater detail, one would need to consult a tax specialist.

A Trust is not a means to hide assets from the South

African Revenue Services. There are laws that prevent Trusts being exploited for tax avoidance purposes. For example, Section 7 C of the Income Tax Act was enacted to close potential loopholes, including interest-free loans.

INCOME TAX

The Trustees are required to register the Trust with the South African Revenue Services (SARS). The Income Tax Act 58 of 1962 requires that the receipt or accrual of income be declared by the Trust for income tax purposes.

Any income received by the Trust is taxed at a flat rate of 45% from Rand one and no rebates apply. Income tax returns for the Trust must be submitted to SARS for annual assessment (from 1 March to 28 February), so it is important to have a reliable accountant or bookkeeper keeping track of transactional inflows and outflows.

However, the Trustees may choose to apply the conduit principle and shift the tax burden to the Beneficiaries, who will be personally liable for the income tax on a sliding scale that ranges between 18% and 45%. This system allows the income to 'flow through' the Trust to the Beneficiaries and negates any Trust liability for income tax.

The law allows a Trust to distribute to Beneficiaries certain amounts per annum, tax-free in their hands. The amounts vary by age, with the advantage going to senior citizens.

- Each Beneficiary up to age 65, qualifies for an amount of R83 100.00 per annum, tax free.
- 65 to 75 years = R128 650.00 per annum, tax free.

- 75 years and over = R143 850.00 per annum, tax free.

This amount may be split over a year or delivered as a single payout.

Most Beneficiaries welcome the income to supplement living expenses and as individuals, they generally pay less tax than the Trust would. Unless it is a significant amount of money, they are unlikely to be taxed at 45%. (The rates of tax may be different for high-net-worth individuals.)

The Trustees also have the discretion to pay the income to the Beneficiaries indirectly, for instance, by paying education fees on their behalf. This could be at the behest of a Beneficiary or as a mechanism to prevent reckless squandering of Trust funds. Trusts are very useful for protecting people from themselves!

CAPITAL GAINS TAX

The Trust is liable for Capital Gains Tax on any Trust property sold, at a rate of 45% *on 80% of the gain* (which equates to an effective rate of 36%). This can also be mitigated with the conduit principle if the Trustees vest the gain in the Beneficiaries (gains acquired in the same tax year), who would then be liable to pay a rate of between 7.5% and 18%, dependent on their tax rate.

If the Beneficiary is a non-resident, the Trust becomes liable for the capital gains tax.

TRANSFER DUTY

This is levied on immovable property. If a property is sold by the Founder (during his or her lifetime) to the Trust, capital gains tax will be payable. Transfer duty will be payable by the Trust.

If such property (like a house) is inherited via a Trust, it remains the property of the Trust unless the Beneficiary chooses to transfer the property into his or her own name. In this case, they are exempt from transfer duty up to the third generation of consanguinity to the Founder (that is, bloodline). However, they will need a conveyancer to process the transfer for registration at the Deeds Office.

Transfer duty, if applied, is on a sliding scale related to the purchase price of the property.

ESTATE DUTY

Without a trust, estate duty is applied at a rate of 20% on a natural person's deceased estate valued *up to R30 million*. From R30 000 001 upwards, the rate of tax applied is 25%. Estate duty is applied to the Testator's estate on his or her death, and the Beneficiaries receive what is left.

A Discretionary Living Trust does not die with the Testator, it remains alive and fully functional. Assuming his or her assets are vested in a Trust, estate duty will not apply to the Trust's assets. That is a saving of at least R200 000 per one million Rand.

DONATIONS TAX

Donations tax, paid by the donor, is levied at the flat rate of 20% on a natural deceased person's estate, *up to R30 million*. Thereafter, it is increased to 25%, that is, from R30 000 001.

An annual donations tax exemption of R100 000.00 per person is allowed for each tax year. Since the exemption is not cumulative, it is important to utilise it annually. Fiscal prudence would suggest either a structured investment plan and/or a donation to a Trust.

Spouses may make donations to one another, irrespective of value, and enjoy exemption from donations tax. So, should spouse A, in any given tax year, not have R100 000.00 available to donate to a third party (like a Trust), spouse B is able to make a donation of R100 000.00 to spouse A, without incurring any penalties or breaking any laws. Spouse A can then make the R100 000.00 donation to a third party. If the third party is a Family Trust, it will derive the benefit of a R200 000.00 tax-free donation. This optimises tax exemption on three fronts.

- No donations tax when spouses donate funds one to the other.
- No donations tax on a R100 000.00 donation per person, per year to a third party, like a Trust.
- Donations made to a Trust no longer form part of an Estate, therefore the amounts donated will not attract estate duty when the donor dies.

A distribution from a Discretionary Living Trust to

Beneficiaries, irrespective of the amount, is exempt from donations tax.

SECONDARY TIER CORPORATIONS TAX (OR DIVIDENDS TAX)

Companies or close corporations offer inadequate asset protection. Assets owned by either entity, such as shares or property, are at risk because they are exposed to creditors. Assets owned by a Trust, are not.

Consider the cost perspective. If an individual wishes to take money from his or her company for personal use (that is, pay him or herself a dividend), the extraction fee alone is 20%. Add the capital gains and income tax borne by the company or close corporation, and one might blanch at the impact of taxes on the original amount. For example:

Per R100.00: Less income tax at 28% (R28.00) = R72.00. Less 20% dividend tax extraction cost (R14.40) = R57.60

To get R57.60 out per R100.00 of the total income is worth some serious reconsideration!

Cost efficiencies may include tax deductions on property rentals, or applying the conduit principle to a Trust. The essential disability and asset protection components would also provide greater peace of mind, both personally and professionally, and a clearly defined succession plan would plot the way forward to prevent interruption in business flow and function, or negative impact on employees.

The inevitability of tax often provides much fodder for discontent, but the reality is that all governments apply taxes to gain revenue. There are avenues individuals can explore that legitimately mitigate the burden. A Tax Specialist or Estate Planning expert is best qualified to assist with the plan.

16.
MARRIAGE AND DIVORCE

A tricky topic. After all, who wants to begin a marriage where a possible end is considered before it has even begun? It may seem self-defeating, but the stitching that holds the best fairy tale together has the potential to lose tensile strength, and unravel over time and under trying circumstances.

Marriage is a law of contract, not equity. The whole concept of traditional marriage roles underwent a seismic shift when the law began to see the historical status quo differently. Not without controversy, the introduction of more gender equitable tenets of law has sought to remedy the bias.

South African law looks at two separate periods of time – pre-and-post-1984. In each section, we shall examine the role of Trusts as a mechanism to protect assets from creditors, or spouses in the event of divorce.

It is important to note that a Trust can only be created when there is nothing threatened, expected or contingent. Therefore, a Trust cannot be created as an emergency response to an impending divorce.

Discretionary Living Trusts are best set up before the parties enter into a marriage contract with each other, so that the financial protection mechanisms of each party are in place at the outset. Dealing with financial affairs upfront will help get one of the key dissention drivers out of the way before the marriage is formalised.

However, parties who are already married and wish to protect their personal assets from potential plunder by creditors or each other, are advised to create Trusts for themselves as individuals, providing they are in agreement.

MARRIAGES CONCLUDED PRE-1984

Couples had two choices: they could marry in Community of Property, or out of Community of Property with an Ante-Nuptial Contract.

Community of Property

Community of Property gave the husband marital power over his wife. Unhappily, as many can attest, this proved prejudicial to the home-based marital partner because marriage in Community of Property is, in principle, based on sharing. Sharing of assets is one thing, sharing of liabilities is quite another. Whilst this sharing may exclude certain assets (such as an inheritance that stipulates it should be excluded from the joint estate), the sharing is of a *joint estate*. Since the joint estate is comprised of both spouses' entire pre-and-post-marital assets *and liabilities* (regardless of which spouse acquired them), one can see the potential risks should divorce or creditors enter the picture.

How, then, might this risk be mitigated?

As partners married in Community of Property, they could agree to create two Discretionary Living Trusts (one each) as part of an estate plan and move select assets out the joint estate and into their individual Trusts, so that those assets would be better protected in the event of divorce, because only those assets and liabilities left in the joint estate would be split down the middle. The assets in the individual Trusts would also be safe from claims by the other party and from creditors.

In effect, moving assets out of a joint estate and into two separate Discretionary Living Trusts represents a restructuring of their respective estates. Their assets will be legally separated and beyond the reach of each other, and creditors.

Ante-nuptial contract

Ante-nuptial contract (out of Community of Property) allows for the complete separation of property. Each spouse owns and controls his or her own estate independently of the other. Nothing is lost or shared if the marriage is terminated, whether accumulated before or during the marriage.

However, it became evident to law makers that this arrangement had the potential to prejudice stay-at-home spouses and so, the redistribution of assets was introduced. It is governed by the Divorce Act 70 of 1979 and can be applied only to civil marriages, not customary marriages.

Typically, in the event of divorce, the spouse making the application for the redistribution order may not have made a material contribution to the marriage coffers because their contribution might have been indirect in nature – that is, the rendering of services related to domestic management (rearing children, controlling family budgets, keeping the house clean and so on) while the other spouse was able to grow his estate through gainful employment. A redistribution order may also apply to a spouse who has contributed materially but not necessarily equally, either in terms of money or property, to the increase of the other's estate during the marriage. Either way, their contribution must have had a positive effect on the other's estate for the court to consider a just and equitable redistribution order.

How might a Discretionary Living Trust be advantageous in this instance, before the accrual system was introduced?

Firstly, as individuals, depending on the extent of their respective assets, they might create their own Trusts to protect their assets from each other in the event of divorce or creditor claims. Secondly, if they bequeath their assets through the Trusts, those assets may not be part of a redistribution order, provided the Trust has been properly created, structured and managed.

MARRIAGES CONCLUDED POST-1984

A new element of fairness was introduced through the Matrimonial Property Act 1984. This law of equity sought to introduce the accrual system and abolish the customary marital power of a gender-based social structure. Generally, unless requested to the contrary by the parties involved, the accrual system is automatically applied to all civil marriages entered into out of community of property, after 1 November 1984.

Individuals who marry by ante-nuptial contract have the choice of including or excluding the accrual benefits. Accrual was introduced to protect the more economically vulnerable spouse from economic prejudice.

Without accrual means that a home-based spouse does not get to share in the economically active spouse's wealth. This affords the economically active spouse the opportunity to grow his or her wealth without the burden of having to share in the event the marriage is terminated. As amoral as it may appear, this spouse may choose to move whatever sum of money or assets he or she has amassed into a Trust. This then, puts those assets beyond the reach of an aggrieved spouse, (a) because they are in Trust and, (b) the contract excludes accrual. It also puts those assets out of the reach of creditors.

With accrual means that while each spouse has and controls his or her pre-and-post-marital assets and liabilities, on termination of the marriage, the spouse whose estate gained less during the course of the marriage, has the right to claim and receive half of the difference between the accruals of their respective estates. It is suggested that assets held in a trust are protected and considered off limits with respect to accrual calculations *providing* those assets were initially included as part of an estate plan and not as a measure to dodge (defraud) the accrual calculation in the event of divorce.

Before marrying anyone, the contractual options need to be explored in depth by both parties, together or separately. Going into marriage believing love will prevail in all circumstances is both immature and ill-advised. When the going gets tough, the concept of fairness is more frequently aligned with what is 'deserving' – and 'deserving' becomes the ugliest battleground. Have it in writing and make sure you understand your options very clearly before you commit to anything. You cannot change the contract after you are married.

To recap your post-1984 marriage contractual options are:

1. In Community of Property (with no marital power).
2. By Ante-Nuptial contract (without accrual).
3. By Ante-Nuptial contract (with accrual).

Better still, go to an Estate Planning specialist and get advice on (a) marriage contracts and (b) the creation of Discretionary Living Trusts as part of an estate plan for a newly married couple. It must be structured properly and fairly to cover both parties in the event the marriage turns sour. A Trust cuts through the emotion and maps the way forward in fine detail – whether the marriage endures, or not.

17.
A DISCRETIONARY LIVING TRUST VERSUS A WILL (TESTAMENTARY) TRUST

A Discretionary Living Trust comes to life during the Founder's lifetime and gets down to business as soon as it has been registered at the Master's offices and the Trustees have been authorised.

A Will Trust is created by a clause in a Will and only comes into effect when the Testator dies. The estate has to be wound up before named Beneficiaries may receive benefits from the Trust. Reminder: creditors take precedence in the queue. The benefits of the Discretionary Living Trust outweigh those of a Will Trust, as detailed below.

1. **Protection.**
a) Assets held in a Discretionary Living Trust are protected from third parties, such as creditors. Once assets are transferred into the Trust, they are owned

by the Trustees.

b) Succession plans are secure. With the Trustees in charge and legally bound to follow the prescripts of the Trust Deed, challenging the Founder's choices is very difficult.

c) Protection in the event the Founder is affected by physical or mental incapacitation during his or her lifetime. Physical injuries or a terminal illness may require serious and protracted medical intervention that disables the Founder for a period of time. The Trust Deed will have mandated the Trustees to manage his or her affairs as he or she determined in the Trust Deed. In the event of mental incapacitation, the same principle applies, circumventing curatorship and its potential risks.

2. **Adherence with flexibility.** Changes sometimes become necessary to cater for unforeseen circumstances. The Trustees, as administrators of the Discretionary Living Trust, have the discretionary powers to effect changes they believe are in the best interests of the Trust property and Beneficiaries.

3. **Saves time and reduces frustration.** Since a Discretionary Living Trust is not governed by the death of the Founder, all the inherent delays, extended waiting period for funds to be released, frustration and desperation become irrelevant. Because the process is smoother and faster, it is also less disruptive and traumatic for the family.

4. **Facilitates administration of assets in other countries.** The process of disposing of property in

other countries is less complicated.

5. **Protects privacy.** A Will Trust is linked to one's estate and the estate is a matter of public record, so any sensitive financial and personal information contained in the Will is open to public scrutiny and having access to information regarding the estate may lead to a claim against it. A Discretionary Living Trust, by comparison, is not linked to a Will so it avoids that situation altogether and remains the property of the Trustees. Property held in a Discretionary Living Trust can be dealt with immediately as it falls outside the Administration of Estates Act 66 of 1965.

6. **Is better protected from attack.** The more comprehensively a Discretionary Living Trust is structured, the more difficult it is to attack. Will Trusts, by comparison, have fewer legal protection mechanisms at their disposal, which creates more opportunity for litigation.

7. **Better results.** The outcomes of legacy planning via a Discretionary Living Trust are much more constructive.

8. **Tax benefits.** Gifts and donations made from a Discretionary Living Trust do not attract the same taxes as Will Trusts. The tax breaks of a Discretionary Living Trust favour the Beneficiaries.

9. **Business continuity planning.** In cases where the Founder would like a business to continue without interruption after his or her passing, a Discretionary Living Trust is a legal instrument that will facilitate 'business as usual'.

10. **Caters for long-and-short-term plans.** A Discretionary Living Trust ensures the continuity and implementation of plans.

11. **There is no waiting period for the Discretionary Living Trust to receive the assets.** Assets set aside for the creation of a Will Trust only become available when the Testator dies, and are transferred into the Trust once the Liquidation and Distribution account has been approved, advertised, and concluded by the Master of the High Court.

12. **Discretion.** Assets in a Discretionary Living Trust are distributed to the Beneficiaries *at the discretion of the Trustees*, a condition which prevents reckless behaviour. Beneficiaries of a Will Trust may do what they like with their inheritance when they receive it.

Trusts have long been considered an old-fashioned, expensive, and complicated solution to protecting the funds of the rich. Trusts are not exclusive to the rich; in fact Discretionary Living Trusts have become something of a revolution. They are more widely accessible to many more people, hardworking folk with commendable work and family ethics who have been squirrelling away their savings for years. Their worth may not amount to multi-millions, but they do want their future and that of their families to be cared for in the most secure, loving and expedient way, especially after they die.

18.
THE POTENTIAL SHORTFALLS OF A WILL

Wills on their own have certain drawbacks. We understand that costs – both in creating the Will and ultimately winding up the Estate – are a key decision driver. But what if you knew of a way that could potentially mitigate certain costs, taxes, and delays after you die and allow your family immediate access to the inheritance you bequeathed to them?

Ignorance should never be a factor when it comes to drawing up a Will. You are urged to research your options so that you understand the consequences of your choices *before* you decide (or die).

Some people blindly follow historical family protocols. Others think, 'What the heck, I'll be dead, so I really don't care!' – and then there are others who would prefer to make it as uncomplicated and stress-free as possible for their heirs. Which are you?

Whilst a Will is created to make provision for the distribution of your assets when you die, there is a significantly more efficient mechanism. Ponder these points:

1. A Will offers no asset or disability protection for you while you are alive.

2. A Will requires the Executor you appointed to begin the laborious process of winding up your Estate through the Master of the High Court.

   - If you have appointed a trusted family member or friend as your Executor, is he or she of steely resolve and familiar with the legal processes? Yes, you may save Executor fees but for the uninitiated, it can be a minefield of red tape, of finding elusive documents and following a maze of unfamiliar legal processes. Ticking multiple boxes takes time and patience and the Master's office is consistently under pressure, which can affect efficiency. It may take one to three years to complete the process, depending on the complexities of the Will and the Estate.

   - If a financial institution assisted in the creation of your Will, they also wind it up for you and subtract their Executor fees from the gross value of your Estate at 3.5% + VAT: e.g. per R1 million (x 3.5% = R35 000 + R5 250 VAT = R40 250) Most Executors work from a Progress Sheet that contains many sections and sub-sections of requirements that need to be met. The process is painstaking, and whilst there is no doubt that the fee is hard earned, it is still a significant chunk out of one's Estate!

   - Your passing may also trigger Capital Gains Tax + Estate Duty. Numerous parameters apply to many variables so these must be accurately calculated.

3. It is easier for a third party to challenge a Will.

4. Assets in other countries may have to be wound up in that country.

THE DISCRETIONARY LIVING TRUST OPTION

This alternative is quite revolutionary. It entails structuring a Will and a Discretionary Living Trust that work in harmony to your advantage, even while you are alive. *Mental incapacitation is particularly difficult if all you have is a Will.* In this instance, a Power of Attorney is deemed invalid and a Curator will be appointed by a judge to handle your affairs. The consequences could be disastrous.

If you have a Will *and* a Discretionary Living Trust, a Curator may be avoided as the Trustees of the Discretionary Living Trust will simply follow the instructions of the Deed you drew up with your attorney, accountant or fiduciary consultant. Access to money need not be a problem providing your assets are in the Trust, so that when you die, the Trust will live on. This circumvents the involvement of the Master's office altogether. Everything continues smoothly and expediently.

Apart from the convenience and ease of flexibility during life and beyond, a Discretionary Living Trust:

- Also provides for asset and disability protection.
- Saves Executor fees (they no longer apply).
- Offers greater protection from potential third-party

attacks.

- Dispenses with Estate-related complications associated with assets in other countries.

A Discretionary Living Trust Centred Plan is so much more straightforward when you die, and yields results faster for the benefit of the heirs. If you seriously consider the cost-to-benefit ratio, a Discretionary Living Trust is the better option.

End-of-life contingencies are never pleasant to talk about, but reality requires that we do. An empowered legacy is way better than a complicated Will littered with hoops and heartache!

Research how a Discretionary Living Trust could best be structured alongside your Will because it is strategic in intent and clearly detailed to ease the angst of the people you leave behind.

19.
SEVEN REASONS WHY CURATORSHIP SHOULD BE AVOIDED

Curatorship has the potential to be troublesome. Planning for life's curve balls is not easy. You need to consider multiple contingencies, however unpleasant or remote they may seem at the time. Otherwise, you may rue the day you did not pay attention when you had the opportunity.

If you (as an adult) are declared mentally incompetent by a medical specialist, the Power of Attorney you signed for someone you trust will have as much legal clout as your children's favourite bedtime story. And if the costs of setting up a Trust scared you, brace yourself for the court costs required to set up (or dismantle) curatorship. You will find yourself with fewer rights than a minor.

Say your mental incapacitation is temporary, you have a severe depression or PTSD episode that renders you incapable of functioning normally for a specific period, that Power of Attorney is useless. A Curator will need to be appointed.

Papers to appoint a Curator will have to be drawn up by an attorney and taken to Court by an advocate. If the judge is satisfied, he or she will appoint a Curator *ad litem* (an interim Curator) to find a suitable permanent candidate to act as Curator of your affairs. A judge will then be required to approve the choice made by the Curator *ad litem*, providing the candidate is prepared to accept the task. The Curator will be remunerated for the performance of his or her duties, typically a percentage of your capital, and prescribed tariffs will apply on income received and/or distributed.

How is this calculated? If, for instance, you have R10 million in capital and R8 million in debt, which figure do you think will determine the fees? If you guessed the difference (that is, R2 million), you are deluded. It would be based on the R10 million. Add the legal and Curator fees to your medical expenses and ponder the escalating costs for a moment...

Here are *some* of the realities of the Court Order given to the Curator/Curatrix if you are the patient:

1. Consent to *any medical or surgical* treatment you may need.
2. Your *detention* in or removal to *any hospital* or *similar institution*.
3. To receive, take care of, control and administer *all* your assets.
4. To carry on or *discontinue*, subject to any law which may be applicable, any trade, business or undertaking of yours.
5. To let, exchange, partition, alienate and for any lawful purpose to *mortgage* or *pledge* any property belonging you, or in which you have an interest.

6. To *incur expenditure* in respect of the improvement of any property you own by means of building or otherwise.

7. To *expend any moneys* belonging to you on the maintenance, education or advancement of *any relative* of yours or *any other person* wholly or partially dependent on you, to continue such acts of bounty or charity exercised by you as the Master, having regard to the circumstances and the value of your Estate, considers reasonable.

Despite the Court's best intentions at the time of appointment, some Curators are better than others. Should any breach of trust occur, or competency levels come into question, the Court (on application) and the Master (in certain circumstances and in terms of the Administration of Estates Act 66 of 1965) has the power to have him or her removed. However, the Curator in question has the right to oppose any assertion of misconduct or incompetency and tie you up in a protracted legal battle while you, perhaps now recovered, have no access to any of your assets. Your fate will lie in the hands of strangers.

To put it bluntly, you are up the proverbial creek, minus a paddle.

What is the alternative?

While you have all your faculties, accept that the above scenario could become a reality one day, particularly if dementia or Alzheimer's runs in your family. Pre-empt the potential disaster and think about putting your assets into a Discretionary Living Trust. It will dispense with the crisis of having a stranger in full control of your affairs and assets and will cost less in the long run. Prioritise the protection of your assets and quality of care you would like to receive if you are mentally incapacitated at any stage.

Find a specialist to answer all your questions and devise a more secure solution that will see you in the hands of people you trust – personally and financially. The tailored alternative of setting up a Discretionary Living Trust will negate this potentially disempowering scenario and provide peace of mind.

20.
WINDING UP AN ESTATE WITH A WILL

Since death is inevitable, you will probably have given some thought to who-you-would-like-to-have-what, when you die.

For that to materialise, you need a Will. This is a document that clearly stipulates what should happen to your Estate when you die. An Estate refers to all the assets (material wealth) and liabilities (debts) you have acquired during your lifetime. Without a Will, your 'who-should-get-what' ideal will be buried with you.

In the absence of a Will, the law of intestate succession will apply. The law holds that any assets should be distributed according to *proven* blood line. Yes, even renegade siblings and offspring!

All estates have to be wound up through the applicable regional Master's office, each of which handles Deceased Estates, Liquidations (Insolvent Estates), Registration of Trusts, Tutors and Curators and the Administration of the Guardian's Fund. They are extremely busy. Consequently, urgency is more of a stretch than a reality.

How long would your family be able to hold out without access to the funds left to them in your Will? The knock-on effect of inadequate financial planning will be felt hardest by those you leave behind.

HOW TO CREATE A WILL

It is better to have your Will drafted by a specialist as it has to comply with certain statutory requirements found in the Wills Act 7 of 1953, and ambiguity must be avoided.

I strongly advise you to have your Will drafted by a professional Estate Planner. I mention this because they have the requisite *depth of knowledge* across *multiple disciplines.* They focus on the most cost-effective and expedient outcomes for the client. Whilst the Will is a vital component to any estate plan, the distribution of assets can be separated from the Will so that they avoid any hold up at the Master's office. No rocket science is required – the uninterrupted flow of financial support to your family versus one to three years waiting for an Estate to be wound up.

An Estate Planning Specialist will also know how to balance the tax implications in your favour. And, the consultation fee is levied at an hourly rate, which is likely to be a fraction of the executor's wealth-based fee of 3.5 percent of the gross value of your estate + VAT, when you die.

WHAT IS THE ROLE OF AN EXECUTOR?

It is advisable to nominate an Executor when drafting the Will. This person will administer and wind up your Estate after you die. It is a matter of personal choice, one that often depends on the complexity of the Estate. Winding up an Estate is quite a rigmarole, especially if all one's assets are vested in the Estate, rather than a Discretionary Living Trust. To the uninitiated, the process can be quite daunting.

Nominating a family member or friend to act as Executor:

Advantages: One might save the Executor fees of 3.5 % on the gross value of the estate + VAT, or a portion of it.

Disadvantages: Lay people may find themselves ill-equipped to manage the minefield of red tape, of finding documents and following a maze of unfamiliar legal processes. It is both time-consuming and onerous, because it involves working with busy officials at the Master of the High Court's offices where unexpected hurdles like backlogs or absenteeism could cause inconvenient delays and considerable frustration.

Nominating a specialist (ask your Estate Planner to recommend a competent deceased estates attorney) to act as Executor:

Advantages: They know exactly what is required, are familiar with the process and work from comprehensive checklists. They are also likely to have fostered co-operative relationships within the system.

Disadvantages: Costs. The upside is that the fee can be negotiated upfront with the agent acting as Executor. This individual may agree to a flat rate or lower percentage, depending on the value and complexity of your Estate.

WHO IS NOT FIT TO ACT AS AN EXECUTOR?

Avoid unrehabilitated insolvents, minors and anyone with a criminal record or diminished mental capacity.

WHAT DOES THE ADMINISTRATIVE PROCESS ENTAIL?

The Executor's checklist for a typical Estate would include:

- Acquiring relevant information, documents and signatures from the relatives – the original Will, identity document of the deceased and all his or her policies, certificates (death, investments and shares) – with regular updates thereafter.
- Safekeeping of any firearms until transferred to the relevant Beneficiary.
- Reporting the Estate to the Master with supportive documents – the death notice, an inventory of the deceased's known assets and their estimated value, the original Will and the Executor's acceptance of trust. Letters of Executorship are issued by the Master once he is satisfied that all is in order.
- Placing the notice to creditors in the Government Gazette and a local newspaper (the newspaper circulated in the area in which the deceased lived at the time of his or her death).
- Opening files for correspondence and essential documents.
- Opening a temporary savings bank account for the Estate.

- Sending letters to creditors and debtors to determine claims for and against the Estate.
- Obtaining valuations of movable and immovable assets.
- Completing and submitting an income tax return to SARS.
- Preparing and submitting the liquidation and distribution account.
- Paying outstanding debts, any estate duties owed and the Master's fees.
- Paying Beneficiaries that which is due to them.
- Fulfilling the Master's final requirements.

WHAT IF YOU NEED TO CHANGE YOUR WILL?

For as long as you are alive, your Will can be changed. Any amendments, to be legal and hold up in Court if challenged after one has passed, need to be recorded legally. Usually, one would go back to whoever created the Will and either create a new Will or prepare a Codicil which allows for minor changes like additions, deletions, or changes to an existing provision. Co-signatories are required as witnesses at the time of signing the Will (and any subsequent amendments) to corroborate the authenticity of the Testator, the person whose Will it is.

HOW CAN YOU PROTECT YOUR CHILDREN SHOULD YOU DIE UNEXPECTEDLY?

It is not uncommon for the surviving spouse to remarry. Neither is it uncommon for the newly acquired spouse to assume that access to any wealth is part of the deal.

The problem is that newly enamoured widows and widowers can be persuaded to do almost anything, while other marriage prospects simply bulldoze their way in, lay claim to and assume control of the wealth *you* worked so hard to accumulate for the exclusive benefit of *your* successors.

Would you not want to prioritise your children's care and protect them financially from such amoral opportunists? The best way to achieve this is to give control of your assets to people you trust and place the assets out of reach of presumptuous third parties. To achieve this, you need to move your assets out of your Estate and into a Discretionary Living Trust.

Timing is of paramount importance in order to optimise current investment opportunities and minimise the tax consequences.

Why impose unnecessary suffering on your family when a solution exists?

Winding up an Estate is complicated; it takes time and diligence because it involves multiple legal processes and role players. Simplify everything. When your assets are in a Discretionary Living Trust and controlled by Trustees:

- You may be granted access to the assets while you are alive.
- There is no waiting for funds to be released to your family when you die.
- Your assets are protected from opportunists.

- Your legacy will continue unhindered.
- Your passing will not incur estate duty.

Act on it now, it is incumbent on individuals to record their desired legacy in a Will and through a Discretionary Living Trust.

It is a responsibility that bears the hallmark of love, gratitude and peace of mind for you and your family.

21.
TIPS:
HOW TO FIND A
QUALIFIED ESTATE
PLANNER

There is a common misconception that all Estate Planners are equal in terms of qualification and expertise. This is not true, any more than it is for the medical fraternity or professional athletes. For example, what would be the likelihood of an Olympic shotput champion winning the 100-metre sprint?

Different disciplines within any profession require precision and dedication to a particular skill honed over years of focus and practice. Therefore, it stands to reason; specialists offer above-average expertise and are the best people to get the job done properly. Their depth of knowledge is reflected in the quality of their services.

However, experience is not necessarily a guiding principle, nor does it automatically engender wisdom. The key question to ask yourself is: 'Will this person have *my* best interests at heart?' because sometimes, lower fees are used to attract higher work volumes which are made possible through cost-saving shortcuts. Some unspecialised practitioners may be tempted to download online templates and use them to cobble together an estate plan that may look impressive on paper but is unlikely to provide the full range of benefits or protection. It may not even hold up in Court if legally challenged. Estate Planning is about a lot more than filling in blanks on reams of paper and any ineptitude could cost you dearly!

Clients looking for an effective Estate Planner should strive for more secure, lasting benefits over short-term gain.

The key characteristics of good Estate Planner:

- The client's interests come first.
- Has a reputation for being ethical.
- Is very knowledgeable and takes pride in his or her work.
- Has been diligent in staying legally current through research, study and contact with other relevant legal bodies.
- Is properly organised to deliver services and documents in a timely manner.
- Has built professional relationships with similarly specialised colleagues and is prepared to seek their advice, if necessary.
- Has amassed a client base of repeat business.
- Is focused and polite.
- Will make you feel comfortable and reassured.
- Is willing to discuss fees upfront (which are usually based on the complexity of the estate plan).
- Has a website that is professional, relevant, informative and updated regularly.

Legal experts come at a price, but the cost pales into insignificance when balanced with the potential tax savings extrapolated over any number of years. Since Estate Planning is highly technical, look for practitioners who have mastered this complicated discipline and have the track record to prove it.

The fruit lies in the detail and whilst experts may also use templates, they have been personally drafted and refined over many years of attending professional Estate Planning seminars, thousands of hours spent poring over relevant legal literature and staying up to date with prevailing legislation as well as lecturing to relevant industry groups. They have earned the reputation of 'specialist', they take their work very seriously and pride themselves in their fastidious attention to detail because the client comes first.

Shopping for price over quality is one of the sorriest mistakes one can ever make.

The estate planner-client relationship is a unique bond based on trust, respect and understanding. It is established through sound listening skills from both parties because no two estate plans are the same:

- Client to estate planner is core to the planner gleaning the full measure of the client's situation, concerns and wishes so that the estate plan can be tailored to fit the client. This will require thorough preparation on the client's part, so that they ask the right questions and receive full, satisfactory answers.
- Similarly, estate planner to client provides the opportunity to ask the sort of questions that will

lead to full understanding of the client's objectives. It is incumbent on the estate planner to ensure that the client understands the professional advice offered in terms of the aforementioned criteria and the implications thereof (legal, financial and personal) and that will allow the client to decide which strategies will work best for them.

You (the client) should leave with a lot to mull over and digest. It is perfectly acceptable to ask your attorney, accountant, stockbroker, insurance agent or financial planner to weigh in on the matter and provide their input so that you obtain some additional perspective. In all dealings, integrity and competency remain the fundamental principles.

What about Estate Planning packages offered by professionals who are not attorneys or estate planners?

However well-intended, they may cause you unnecessary taxes and expenses or make innocent mistakes that inadvertently disqualify you from major exemptions, deductions and credits. And, the plan is unlikely to meet your specific needs. Again, generic templates may not be sufficiently client-specific and any mistakes or deficiencies may only come to light when you die.

To be effective and successful, an estate plan has to:

- Perform a comprehensive analysis of the client's assets and personal financial situation with due consideration given to the client's personal goals, hopes and aspirations. This analysis serves as the motherboard from which all the planning and detail will flow.

- Create, develop and implement the client's short-, medium- and long-term financial planning goals.
- Protect the client's assets from third-party attack.
- Make provision for amendments without requiring a major redraft at vast cost to the client.
- Ensure financial continuity for his or her Beneficiaries after the client's death.

Estate planning is not a one-off transaction, it is the beginning of a long-term relationship as circumstances change and Trusts need to be revisited regularly. Make sure you enjoy spending time with the estate planner (that is, an attorney, accountant or fiduciary consultant) of your choice and that the relationship fosters complete peace of mind.

22.
BLENDED FAMILIES

Human beings, as a rule, find a solitary life quite unsettling. The desire to connect with another is a strong driver behind second marriages, and the reconnect can be hugely rewarding. It can also be complicated because the new relationship may be strongly nuanced by past experience and accompanied by someone else's children.

So, when it comes to wanting to commit to one another, finances become a core component. Most people want to provide for their spouse and children as their resources permit, so the discussion about finances needs to be honest and open, strategic and sensible. It may well prove to be a barometer test of the health of your relationship because it could degenerate into a spat based on expectations and demands, or capitulation blinded by new love. Neither is helpful!

This is a new partnership, two people creating a fresh start and financial future that meets their individual and combined family needs. To know what you can leave, you have to know what is yours to leave, so do the homework. What is especially pertinent to blended families, is that each spouse may want to leave property to different Beneficiaries.

To find the most equitable way forward, it is suggested that you enlist the services of an accredited estate planner with proven experience and financial nous. As a neutral party, the planner can cut through the emotion and insecurities and find solutions that meet the needs of both parties, as well as their respective children – current and future.

Step one requires each partner to either update or create a new Will, and then formalise an estate plan that supports the new relationship and benefits the blended family as a brand-new entity. The estate plan should clearly identify the combined extent of the pie (assets and liabilities of both parties), what should be combined and shared, what should be separated to make provision for future contingencies or personal responsibilities (like debt, a widowed mother or a disabled sibling), and what should be under consideration, such as new life assurance policies.

There is no monetary formula to apply, it is a negotiation based on personal wishes, assets and responsibilities. Think about:

- Your own needs and resources.
- The needs and resources of your new spouse.
- The needs of existing children.
- The needs of any future children you may have together.
- The relationship with your stepchildren and what they may need from you.

A core planning issue for blended families is how to

divide one's resources so that children from a previous marriage (or relationship) are not compromised.

The extended life expectancy of a younger spouse has to be factored into the plan, especially if the younger spouse has been encouraged to leave the work force, either to support the older spouse's business endeavours and aspirations, or to run the home. Giving up a good proportion of one's productive working years to care for the family will impact this person's future needs and resources.

Think about what you would like to accomplish in terms of material provision, during your life and after you die. This balancing act should make adequate provision for the new spouse (and corresponding children) and ensure that what is left when this partner dies is shared fairly with your children from a former spouse.

When it comes down to who-should-get-what when you die, blended families are likely to have more parties with a vested interest in their slice of the pie, the perfect recipe for a cross-family feud. To manage expectations and mitigate contentious claims, you need a detailed plan – and Trusts offer the most proactive solution.

What you should strive to prevent:
- The surviving spouse and children competing for funds from a common Trust, or similar source.
- The children having to wait for the surviving spouse to die before they can receive their inheritance.
- Giving full control of your entire estate to your current spouse.
- Accepting a verbal agreement in good faith. Make

sure both parties formalise their financial intentions and plans in a Will and an estate plan, so that there are no cripplingly rude shocks when one party dies.

Should you make provision for your stepchildren?

That depends on the extent of your resources and relationship with them. You may want to make a special bequest to some little person brought into the relationship by your new spouse, a child you have known since he or she was a toddler and have come to love as your own. Conversely, you may not want to leave a cent to the insolent lout you inherited, the one with all the drive and ambition of a retired sloth.

The point is, be mature and plan carefully *at the outset*. Each situation is different, so put all your cards on the table for dissection and discussion. This exercise should help quantify one's assets in order to identify priorities, assist with forward planning and reach agreement.

An estate planner would be of immense value with all the experience and knowledge necessary to steer you in the right direction and formulate a plan that sits comfortably with all concerned.

SUMMARY

When we talk about Wills and Estate Planning, our minds automatically default to death.

Quick, change the subject!

The sooner we tackle reality head on and deal decisively with potential bumps in the road during our life journey and the inevitability of death, the better for all. We aim to break some uncomfortable barriers and highlight consequences relating to poor choices. Most choices have a compounding effect, so the question is, will your choices have a positive or negative effect on your life going forward?

An Estate Plan compels us to think ahead. It is designed to direct and meet our forward-planning goals without being derailed by negative life events. Let's face it, a goal without a plan is about as useful as a bicycle without wheels.

A Discretionary Living Trust is a strategy that optimises life and opportunity, a plan that makes provision for today and all our tomorrows. Just as importantly, it is also a plan designed to protect material wealth from erosion and access by unwelcome third parties.

Some tomorrows may bring more rain than sunshine. In order to reclaim the sunshine, we need to plan for contingencies such as physical disability or the loss of mental acuity. I stress, rather plan for contingencies *your* way instead of having another unsuitable plan thrust upon you.

Opt for smart and sensible choices by staying informed.

Think about wealth protection as well. It is as much about protecting capital growth and enjoying the compounding effect, as it is about preparing for rainy spells.

As an exponent and specialist in Estate Planning and Discretionary Living Trusts, I strongly advise you to explore your options. The situations that have long concerned me are curatorship and the length of time it takes to wind up an estate – both have the potential to cause unnecessary hardship.

A Discretionary Living Trust offers multiple benefits, including the ability to circumvent curatorship and the challenging task of winding up an estate. Its capacity to function as 'business as usual', without any event-related interruptions, is mind blowing.